Birds from North Borneo

by Max C. Thompson

CONTENTS

INTRODUCTION

The major part of this report is an account of birds collected by the expedition of the Bernice P. Bishop Museum of Honolulu, Hawaii, to North Borneo, from June 24, 1962, through January 14, 1963. Most of the time spent in the then British Colony was devoted to collecting in lowland habitats. The chief collecting localities were in the vicinity of Quoin Hill on the Semporna Peninsula, and near Kalabakan. Approximately two weeks were spent in surveying the Tenom area. Additional work was done by the North Borneo Department of Agriculture after my departure, mainly by Antonio D. Garcia.

ACKNOWLEDGMENTS

I am indebted to J. L. Gressitt of the Entomology Department of the Bishop Museum for providing the opportunity for me to work on the expedition and to examine and report on the material collected. Without the help of the North Borneo Department of Agriculture, the success of our expedition would have been restricted. The Entomologist of North Borneo, G. R. Conway, was of great help with our logistic problems as was the Director of the Department, Mr. E. J. H. Berwick, and the Agronomist of Cocoa Research Station, Ed Wyrley-Birch. The Bombay Burmah Trading Corporation, Ltd., provided facilities and transportation at Kalabakan. Mr. Dai Rees of that corporation should be especially mentioned. Others who helped are: J. A. Comber, Ronnie Young, Mr. and Mrs. Horace Traulsen, Maureen Wyrley-Birch, and the Resident, Tawau, Mr. Peter Edge. The Conservator of Forests kindly provided the necessary permits for collecting.

Authorities of the United States National Museum and The American Museum of Natural History generously permitted me to work at those institutions, using their specimens for comparative studies. Other specimens were borrowed from the Museum of Comparative Zoology, Rijksmuseum Van Natuurlijke Historie, British Museum (Natural History), and the Yale Peabody Museum. Dr. Alexander Wetmore, Herbert Deignan, and Charles Vaurie helped with some of the more difficult taxonomic problems. Specimens cited in this report are in the Bernice P. Bishop Museum, The University of Kansas Museum of Natural History, The University of Michigan Museum of Zoology, and the U. S. National Museum.

Richard F. Johnston and Robert M. Mengel kindly read the manuscript and made many helpful suggestions. The latter re-read it and assisted with the editing.

The most recent comprehensive work published previous to my preparation of manuscript for the present account was Smythies (1960) "The Birds of Borneo."

This report is a partial result of field work supported by a grant from the United States Army Medical Research and Development Command, Department of the Army, to the Bernice P. Bishop Museum for research on ectoparasites of vertebrates. The contract numbers were DA-MD-49-193-62-G47 and G65. The Chapman Fund of The American Museum of Natural History met part of the cost of transporting, to and from the United States, specimens from North Borneo collected after I left there.

METHODS

While collecting at Quoin Hill, we used only guns in taking birds. At an area 12 miles north of Kalabakan, we supplemented the guns with mist nets in the primary forest. This method was excellent for taking rarely seen species. For example the thrush Zoothera interpres was never seen in the field but was taken several times in mist nets.

Another method of collecting was the use of native snares. Such snares were made of heavy nylon string tied to a sapling, held down by a nylon string attached to a treadle. When a bird stepped on the treadle, it tripped the snare and a loop closed about its feet, hoisting it aloft. To divert large ground birds and mammals into the snare, natives placed brush barriers along the top of a ridge for one or two miles. Animals were diverted by these barriers until they came to an opening; if they went through they usually tripped the trap. Pheasants and the large ground cuckoo were taken in this manner.

NOTES ON ZOOGEOGRAPHY

The avifauna of Borneo is of Indo-Malayan affinities. The number of birds endemic to Borneo is relatively small; most species are shared with the Asian mainland. Only 29 birds are known to be endemic to the island and 17 of these are montane. The large proportion of montane endemics is not surprising, because Borneo has been connected with the Asian continent in recent geological time; lowland isolation, and differentiation, has been less extensive than the montane. The Sunda Shelf, on which Borneo is situated, lies in a shallow sea generally less than 300 feet deep. Beaufort has shown that the Malay Peninsula, Sumatra, and Java were connected until early historic times (Darlington, 1957:488).

The endemic species in Borneo are members of four, possibly five, genera that are also endemic. Four of these five genera are montane in distribution. The only endemic for which the geographic history cannot be adequately explained is the monotypic Pityriasis gymnocephala. Its affinities seem to be with the Cracticidae of New Guinea and Australia. The species has been found throughout Borneo. Since Pityriasis is endemic to Borneo, it probably was detached from the parent stock at an early period. The Australasian affinities of Pityriasis emphasize its zoogeographical peculiarities. A more detailed discussion of this species appears in the annotated list below.

COLLECTING LOCALITIES AND COLLECTORS

1. Cocoa Research Station, Quoin Hill, elevation 750 feet, Tawau. Max C. Thompson (MCT) and Antonio D. Garcia (ADG). 2. Tawau. Max C. Thompson. 3. Twelve miles north of Kalabakan, elevation 600 feet. Max C. Thompson. 4. Kalabakan, elevation 50 feet. Max C. Thompson. 5. Tiger Estate, 20 miles northwest of Tawau. Max C. Thompson, Antonio D. Garcia. 6. Ulu Balung Cocoa Estate, Mile 27, Quoin Hill, elevation 750 feet, Tawau. Antonio D. Garcia. 7. Karindingen Island. Max C. Thompson. 8. Siamil Island. Max C. Thompson. 9. Lahad Datu. Antonio D. Garcia. 10. Kuala Sumawang, 25 miles west of Sandakan. Antonio D. Garcia. 11. Agricultural Station, Mile 17, Sandakan (Gum-Gum). Antonio D. Garcia. 12. One-fourth mile east Gum-Gum, Sandakan. Antonio D. Garcia. 13. Lamag, Kinabatangan River. Antonio D. Garcia. 14. Pintasan Agriculture Station, Kinabatangan River. Antonio D. Garcia. 15. Kampong Kuamut, Kinabatangan River. Antonio D. Garcia. 16. Kampong Maluwa, Kinabatangan River. Antonio D. Garcia. 17. Ka-Karis, Kinabatangan River, elevation 200 feet. Antonio D. Garcia. 18. Tongod, Kinabatangan River, elevation 300 feet. Antonio D. Garcia. 19. Tuaran. Max C. Thompson, Antonio D. Garcia, S. F. W. Chong (SFWC). 20. Telipok. Antonio D. Garcia, G. R. Conway. 21. Mt. Rumas, 5 miles northwest of Tuaran, elevation 75 feet, Antonio D. Garcia. 22. Five and one-half miles southwest of Tenom, elevation 4,000 feet. Max C. Thompson. 23. Tenom, elevation 600 feet. Max C. Thompson. 24. Kampong Banjar, Mile 29, Keningau. Antonio D. Garcia. 25. Oil Palm Research Station, Mile 32, elevation 40 feet, Sandakan. Antonio D. Garcia.

ECOLOGY OF THE COLLECTING LOCALITIES

QUOIN HILL.--At this locality I recognized five habitat types as follows:

Primary forest.--We were fortunate to be able to work at Quoin Hill because it had been opened to cultivation (of Cocoa, Theobroma cacao) for only a few years. Thus the primary forest here started at the edge of the Cocoa Research Station. This was in marked contrast to areas on the west coast, where one would need to travel many miles inland to find virgin forest. The forest at Quoin Hill was typical tropical rain-forest, composed mostly of dipterocarps (Dipterocarpaceae). These comprise an essentially Indo-Malayan family, members of which are so conspicuous that we commonly referred to it as Evergreen Dipterocarp Forest. The lowland forests of Borneo are composed of approximately 3,000 species of trees (Browne, 1955). At Quoin Hill, as in most of the tropical rain-forest of Borneo, the forest canopy is stratified in three layers, a distinct and easily recognizable top story and less easily separable middle and lower stories. The top canopy is composed of foliage of giant trees that may tower to heights of 200 feet and have trunks three to seven feet in diameter. The trunk is usually unbranched for 50 to 100 feet and the whole tree is supported by buttresses jutting out from the main trunk. Some of the most important plants in the tropical rain-forest are the strangler figs (Ficus sp.). These plants, when in fruit, draw birds in large flocks to feed upon them. Such figs were common about the edges of the research station and some birds taken from these trees were never taken elsewhere. The birds seemed to wait for a certain degree of ripeness of fruits; on one day the figs were unmolested and the next day the trees would be swarming with birds. Strangler fig trees reach tremendous size and help form the upper forest canopy.

The middle and lower forest canopies are not easily separable and I shall speak of them together. The trees forming these varied from 10 to 60 feet in height. The ground surface beneath the trees was usually bare except for leaf litter and dead branches. Sunlight penetrates only where the big trees have been removed or where the larger trees are otherwise widely spaced. At Quoin Hill the large trees of species affording lumber of commercial quality had been taken out, modifying somewhat the character of the forest. Such forest actually contained many of the animals characteristic of primary forest, and I refer to it as badly disturbed primary forest.

Secondary forest.--In some of the areas adjoining the research station, roads had been bulldozed for future expansion and trees had been cut. These areas were starting to grow dense stands of grass and shrubs and will be jungle in a few years unless cut back. Most of the trees in this area are saplings with some trees as large as a foot in diameter.

Fluviatile waters.--There are numerous small streams in the Quoin Hill area, the largest being the Balung River and Apas River. Little work was done along these streams and only the thrushes of the genus Enicurus and some kingfishers seemed to be confined to them.

Cocoa plantations.--Artificial plantings of cocoa, Theobroma cacao, formed a major habitat type at Quoin Hill, and provided a major source of food for birds. Cocoa planters have found it necessary to provide shade with trees of some other species. In some instances trees from the original primary forest were left standing to provide this shade, but more often exotic trees were planted. Most of the shade trees were of no use to birds save for providing resting places. Trema orientalis was the most important in providing food for birds. Its fruit was used more by the frugivorous species of birds than that of any other tree in the cocoa plantings. Tree Cassava, an exotic, was constantly attended by the nectariniids, or honey creepers.

Although the cocoa plantings did not provide much plant material for bird food, they did apparently nourish a horde of insects, which the birds fed upon. A Drongo-cuckoo, Surniculus lugubris, had 50 caterpillars in its stomach. Healthy cocoa trees were sparsely inhabited by birds but areas that were obviously infested with insects literally swarmed with birds. Dead shade trees in the cocoa plantings also provided food for woodpeckers, with four species being found utilizing these dead trees.

Abaca.--The last of the habitat types that I recognized at Quoin Hill was a small grove of Abaca, Musa textilis, and wild bananas, Musa sp. This habitat type was frequented by spiderhunters (Arachnothera sp.) of the family Nectariniidae.

KALABAKAN.--We worked at three localities in this area: 12 miles north of Kalabakan, Brantian Estate, and Kalabakan.

Primary forest.--We were fortunate in being able to work on the very edge of the primary forest 12 miles north of Kalabakan. The composition of the primary forest was much like that at Quoin Hill and will not be discussed further. About a month after we arrived at our forest camp, logging crews moved in and cut the commercial timber near our area. The only immediately noticeable difference in the makeup of the avifauna after destruction of the forest canopy was the appearance of the drongo Dicrurus aeneus. This drongo was seen in areas where the trees had been cut, sitting on limbs and darting out after insects.

Secondary forest.--The area around Kalabakan proper was in secondary forest, which was almost impossible to penetrate. At Kalabakan, Cymbirhynchus macrorhynchus, Cecropsia striolata, and Macronous ptilosus were taken and I did not see them elsewhere. Kalabakan is situated on the Kalabakan River at the upper tidal limit. The Nipa-Mangrove association, not investigated, lies immediately below Kalabakan.

The Brantian Estate area was mostly in secondary forest and was situated on the Brantian River. There were some fairly large areas of grass with water buffalo wallows in them. These grassy areas were favorite haunts of the Painted Quail, Coturnix chinensis.

TENOM.--The first locality that we investigated was 5.5 miles southwest of Tenom, approximately 4,000 feet elevation, in moss forest. A few days were spent collecting in the area of Tenom itself.

Moss forest.--The lower altitudinal limit of the moss forest was about 3,600 feet. The trees on top of the mountain were mostly oaks (Quercus) and were festooned with ferns, orchids, and other epiphytes. The area had been used as a triangulation station by a survey team and a small area on top of the mountain had been cleared earlier. At the time of our visit this small area had grown to secondary vegetation, mostly Pandanus. The oaks in the primary forest surrounding this disturbed area were generally about 30 to 50 feet high and there was little undergrowth in virgin stands. This area was usually swathed in fog from three o'clock in the afternoon until eleven o'clock the next morning. One morning of our fourteen there was clear.

Paddy.--The area visited at Tenom itself consisted mostly of old paddy grown to grass and scrub. Forest did occur but was of secondary nature in the immediate vicinity of Tenom.

SIAMIL ISLAND.--This island is about one mile in circumference and the highest point is about 300 feet above sea level. The island has high bluffs on three sides but slopes gently to the sea on the other. There were patches of forest left on the island, one on the north side and one on the south. The sheer bluffs on the east side of the island were covered with Pandanus sp. The undergrowth of the north forest had been cut, leaving extensive bare areas. The principal undergrowth was rattan. The natives are clearing and planting more of the island to coconuts and hope eventually to clear it completely.

KARINDINGEN ISLAND.--This island, about half a mile in circumference and between 10 and 20 feet above sea level at its highest point, was surrounded by extensive coral reefs and sand; the principal vegetation was mangroves.

ECOLOGICAL AFFINITIES OF THE AVIFAUNA AT QUOIN HILL

More time was spent at Quoin Hill than at any other locality. Fifty five of the more common and hence best-known birds are listed in Table 1 together with their primary and secondary preferences of habitat. The habitat distribution of the birds shows the amount of secondary utilization of habitats by birds that occurred predominantly in one habitat. Cocoa was utilized by 6.2 per cent of the birds of the primary forest, and 88.8 per cent of birds of the secondary forest. This indicates that cocoa is an effective substitute for secondary forest for some birds. Of the species of the primary forest, 18.7 per cent occurred also in secondary forest; thus, three times as many species of primary forest utilized secondary forest as utilized cocoa. This too might be expected, since "secondary" forest is of frequent natural occurrence and an ancient feature while the comparatively simple cocoa plantings are new and artificial.

TABLE 1.--Habitat preferences of 55 Quoin Hill birds.

X = Primary forest   O = Secondary forest

SPECIES	Primary forest	Secondary forest	Cocoa plantations	Fluviatile water	Abaca
Treron curvirostra		X			
Cacomantis merulinus		O	X		
Chalcites malayanus			X		
Phaenicophaeus chlorophaeus		O	X		
Harpactes diardi	X				
Harpactes duvauceli	X				
Alcedo euryzona				X	
Ceyx erithacus	X				
Eurystomus orientalis		X	O		
Calorhamphus fuliginosus		O	X		
Megalaima chrysopogon		X	O		
Megalaima henrici	X		O		
Sasia abnormis	O	X			
Meiglyptes tukki		X			
Dryocopus javensis		X	O		
Chrysocolaptes validus		O	X		
Eurylaimus ochromalus		O	X		
Pitta guajana	X				
Coracina fimbriata			X		
Aegithina viridissima			X		
Chloropsis cyanopogon		X			
Irena puella		X			
Pycnonotus brunneus			X		
Criniger bres		X	O		
Criniger phaeocephalus	X				
Criniger finschii			X		
Hypsipetes criniger		X	O		
Copsychus pyrrhopygus	X				
Copsychus stricklandi		X	O		
Enicurus ruficapillus				X	
Pellorneum capistratum	X				
Trichastoma malaccense	X	O			
Trichastoma sepiarium		X			
Malacopteron magnum	X	O			
Malacopteron magnirostre	X	O			
Kenopia striata	X				
Stachyris poliocephala		X			
Alcippe brunneicauda	X		O		
Orthotomus atrogularis		X			
Orthotomus sepium		X	O		
Rhipidura perlata	X				
Muscicapa dumetoria	X				
Rhinomyias umbratilis	X				
Hypothymis azurea			X		
Anthreptes simplex			X		
Anthreptes rhodolaema			X		
Nectarinia hypogrammica		X			
Arachnothera longirostris					X
Arachnothera flavigaster					X
Arachnothera chrysogenys					X
Arachnothera affinis					X
Zosterops everetti		O	X		
Lonchura fuscans		X	O		
Oriolus xanthonotus		X	O		
Platysmurus leucopterus		X	O		
Total Primary	16				

| 18 | 14 | 2 | 4 | | | | | Total Secondary | 1 | 8 | 14 | 0 | 0 ---------------------
-----+----+----+----+----+----

The avifauna at Quoin Hill was a mixture of montane, submontane, and lowland species. Smythies (1957:527) defines four altitudinal areas of distribution: Higher Montane, Montane, Submontane, and Lowland. Higher Montane birds have not been recorded on mountains the summits of which are lower than 5,000 feet, although on higher peaks the actual lower limit of occurrence may be considerably below 5,000 feet. Montane birds have not been recorded on mountains the summits of which are lower than 3,000 feet, although specimens may have been taken below that altitude on higher peaks. Submontane, as defined by Smythies, is a comprehensive term applied to birds occurring from sea level to an elevation of 5,000 feet but ordinarily not found away from mountainous country. The Lowland birds normally range from sea level to 3,000 feet. Of the 125 species of birds observed at Quoin Hill, 1.6 per cent were Montane, 14.4 per cent were Submontane and 84 per cent were Lowland species. The distribution of birds 12 miles north of Kalabakan closely resembled that at Quoin Hill except for the total absence of Montane species and an increase of Submontane species to 25 per cent. The observation of fewer species (48) can be attributed to the nearly uniform habitat.

The avifauna in the moss forest 5.5 miles southwest of Tenom was unusual in that 45.4 per cent consisted of Lowland species; this locality lies 4,000 feet above sea level, yet only 27.3 per cent of its species were Submontane and 27.3 per cent Montane. If one looks at these figures from the standpoint of the actual importance of the three groups at this place, however, a different picture emerges. Some of the Lowland species were seen only once while I was there and few were common, while all of the Submontane and most of the Montane forms were more or less common.

SEASONALITY OF BREEDING

The breeding season in North Borneo.--Birds in the Quoin Hill area of eastern Borneo seem to breed most commonly in June, July, and August. Table 2 lists 34 of the more common species at Quoin Hill for which evidence on breeding was available. The actual evidence was provided by females with active brood patches or active ovaries, males with enlarged testes, birds in juvenal plumage, or birds actively in annual molt. From such data dates of presumed breeding were extrapolated. In Table 2, the solid black lines indicate dates for which both male and female were in breeding condition. The dotted lines indicate enlarged testes but no evidence of breeding in females. In the bottom line of Table 2, the figures indicate the percentage of the population breeding in any one month. For instance, 2.9 per cent of the birds were breeding in March, but 73 per cent were breeding in June. Rainfall records from the Cocoa Research Station from April, 1959, to December, 1964, were available to me. These data, along with the average for each month, are given in Table 3. There appears to be little correlation between rainfall and breeding season at Quoin Hill. A true dry season in the Quoin Hill area does not occur, but monthly rainfall has varied from 0.57 inches to 21.27 inches in a single year.

TABLE 2.--Seasonality of common breeding birds at Quoin Hill. Solid lines indicate times of occurrence of known breeding; dotted lines represent times of presumed breeding.

```
================================================================
============= SPECIES | J | F | M | A | M | J | J | A | S | O | N | D -------------
----------------+---+---+---+---+---+---+---+---+---+---+---+--- Treron curvirostra | | |
| | | |-----| | | Cacomantis merulinus | | | | | | | | | -----Chalcites malayanus |
| | | | | | -------- | | | | Phaenicophaeus | | | | | | | | | | | | | curvirostris | | | |
| ------------ | | | | Collocalia fuciphaga | | | | | | | ------ | | | | Chaetura
leucopygialis | | | | | | ------| | | | | | Harpactes diardi | | | | | ----------- | | |
Eurystomus orientalis | | | | ---------- | | | | | | Calorhamphus fuliginosus | | |
| | | -----| | Megalaima chrysopogon | | | | | | | | --------- | | | Megalaima
mystacophanes | | | | | | | -| | | Sasia abnormis | | | | | ------- | | | | |
Micropternus brachyurus | | | | | | -------- | | | | | Dryocopus javensis | | | | |-
```

------- | | | | | Pycnonotus cyaniventris | | | | | | | | | -------- | Pycnonotus atriceps | | | --------- | | | | | | | Pycnonotus brunneus | | | | | | ---------------- | | Pycnonotus | | | | | | | | | | | | erythrophthalmus | | | | | | -------- | | | | Zoothera interpres | | | | --------- | | | | | | Malacopteron magnirostre | | | | | --------- | | | | | Ptilocichla leucogrammica | | | | | | ------------ | | | Kenopia striata | | | | | ------- | | | | Stachyris maculata | | | | | ----------| | | | | Orthotomus atrogularis | | | | | | ----------------- | | Orthotomus sericeus | | | | | | ------------- | | | Orthotomus sepium | | | | | | ---------------- | | Rhipidura perlata | | | | |-------- | | | | | Prionichilus xanthopygius | | | | | | | --------------- Anthreptes rhodolaema | | | | | | --------- | | | | Arachnothera flavigaster | | | | | | | | | | ------ Pityriasis gymnocephala | | | | | | | | | | -- -------- Oriolus xanthonotus | | | | | ---------- | | | | Platysmurus leucopterus | | | | | ---------- | | | | +---+---+---+---+---+---+---+---+---+---+---+--- | J | F | M | A | M | J | J | A | S | O | N | D The percentage of breeding +---+---+---+---+---+-- -+---+---+---+---+---+--- in any one month is as | | | | | | | | | | | | follows: | 0 | 0 |2.9|8.8| 38| 73| 58| 50| 35| 17| 11| 8 --------------------------+---+---+--- +---+---+---+---+---+---+---+---+---

Birds in the moss forest near Tenom appeared to be breeding in January, paralleling the trend found by Voous (1950a) for the lowlands of Borneo.

Other Bornean observations.--Voous (1950a) summarized data assembled by Coomans de Ruiter on the breeding of birds in the lowland of western Borneo near Pontianak. It appears that the breeding season in that part of Borneo, and indeed in all of western Borneo (Banks, 1950), starts in December and reaches a peak in March.

TABLE 3.--Monthly rainfall records, Cocoa Research Station, Quoin Hill.

=== =============== Year |Jan. |Feb. |Mar. |April|May |June |July |Aug. |Sept.|Oct. |Nov. |Dec. ------+-----+-----+-----+-----+-----+-----+-----+----+-----+--- --+-----+----- 1959 | | | | 6.49|12.16|11.11| 7.64|12.11| 4.75|

8.33|12.10|13.81 1960 | 9.24| 8.17| 3.76|10.65| 8.84|11.00| 6.31|11.25|
8.56| 5.49| 8.39|11.81 1961 | 6.68| 8.06| 4.35| 4.74| 7.55| 7.25| 5.93|
2.40| 7.47| 5.58| 4.38|10.73 1962 | 3.82| 6.76|13.72| 9.68| 6.82| 7.49|
6.59| 5.82| 7.81| 9.47|19.80| 9.28 1963 |21.27| 8.18| 7.64| 0.57| 5.83|
4.62| 0.64|12.49| 5.24| 8.75| 7.43|11.05 1964 | 4.17| 7.92|
4.40|11.20|11.82| 8.04| 2.42| 7.52| 5.69|13.15| 8.82| 9.88 Avg. | 9.03|
7.81| 6.77| 7.22| 8.83| 8.25| 4.92| 8.59| 6.58| 8.46|10.15|11.09 ------+-----
+-----+-----+-----+-----+-----+-----+-----+-----+-----+-----+-----

Gibson-Hill (1952) has questioned Banks' (1950) interpretation of data from the egg collection of V. W. Ryves. Gibson-Hill has shown that the data collected by Ryves covered two widely separated localities, one at Kiau near Kota Belud and the other near Sandakan. The former locality is on the west coast of North Borneo and the latter on the east coast of North Borneo. Gibson-Hill points out, and rightly so, that the timing of the rainfall in different parts of Borneo must be taken into account because of the large regional variation. The nesting data from the Ryves egg collection are scant and when used alone possibly yield a distorted view of the actual breeding season. Ryves did no collecting in the Sandakan area between September and March, and in the Kiau area between May and January. Although the breeding data from North Borneo accumulated by both Ryves and myself are limited, and records of rainfall are scant, there appears to be a trend toward breeding after the heavy rains have fallen.

Seasonality of breeding in tropical birds.--Possibly Bornean birds breed mostly in the "driest" part of the year. If so, this is in contrast with the time of breeding of birds of other tropical areas. Moreau (1950) found that in the Congo there was no distinct breeding season for most groups of birds, but that in East Africa there was a double breeding season; the peaks coincided with the two rainy seasons. Lack (1950) found that the Geospizinae of the Galapagos breed only when it rains and that rainfall causes a flurry of nest building and singing. If the rains stop, then the courtship activities stop until the next rains. Miller (1963) found that in birds of a western Andean cloud forest the breeding season was spread over the year and that breeding could not be correlated with rainfall.

Obviously more study is required on breeding of birds in Borneo before the timing of the annual cycle can be ascertained.

ACCOUNTS OF SPECIES

The English names used in this report follow Smythies (1960) where possible. If the bird has not been recorded from Borneo previously, then I have resorted to Delacours and Mayr's "Birds of the Philippines" (1946). The taxonomy is that of Smythies (1960), except where current American or my own opinion differs and where new evidence has warranted a change. The sequence of families is that of Wetmore (1960).

Two species listed beyond that had not previously been recorded from the island of Borneo are: Red-footed Booby, Sula sula; and Whitehead's Thick-head, Pachycephala whiteheadi. Six additional kinds listed beyond had not previously been recorded from North Borneo. They are: Chinese Egret, Egretta eulophotes; Knot, Calidris canutus; Ground Cuckoo, Carpococcyx radiceus; Stachyris nigriceps hartleyi; Finch's Bulbul, Criniger finschii; and Pale Blue Flycatcher, Muscicapa unicolor.

=Sula sula= (Linnaeus): Red-footed Booby.--A captive seen in the Tawau police station was said to have been caught when it landed at night on a police launch anchored off Siamil Island in or near May, 1962. The bird was in first-year or second-year plumage, seemed to be tame, and was thriving on a diet of fish. Identification was made by Alexander Wetmore from a photographic print. This is the first seemingly substantiated record of the species from Borneo, although it probably occurs there regularly. The species breeds on Bankoran Island and on Tubbataha Reef in the Sulu Sea (Smythies, 1960:113).

=Fregata ariel= (G. R. Gray): Lesser Frigatebird.--This conspicuous bird on the waters around Tawau is occasionally seen in Cowie Harbor but more often along the coast outside the Harbor. On September 20 an estimated 300-500 birds circled over the shore northeast of Tawau.

=Ardea sumatrana sumatrana= Raffles: Dusky-gray Heron.--Specimens, 2. Karindingen Island: [Male] testis 12 ?23 mm., November 24, 1962, MCT 3308; [Male], November 24, 1962, MCT 3309.

The specimens were taken on the coral sand beach surrounding Karindingen Island. At least 10 were seen feeding on the beach and on a reef. One (MCT 3308) had testes of a size suggesting that it was in breeding condition.

=Casmerodius alba modestus= (Gray): Common Egret.--Specimen, 1. Karindingen Island: [Female], November 24, 1962, MCT 3310.

This species was seen on three dates: August 17 at Karindingen Island, where 30 were observed feeding along the mangroves bordering the island; on November 24, on the same island, where a specimen was taken from a flock of 30 birds that had been feeding on the coral sand and reef; and on November 30 when a single bird landed at the small reservoir at the Cocoa Research Station and began to feed in the shallow water. Only four specimens appear to have been recorded earlier (Smythies, 1957:561), although Smythies (1963:270) lists additional sight records.

=Egretta garzetta= (Linnaeus): Little Egret.--On November 24 at Karindingen Island, I observed several mixing freely with individuals of E. sacra on the coral sand beaches and reefs.

=Egretta eulophotes= (Swinhoe): Chinese Egret.--Specimen, 1: Ka-Karis, Kinabatangan River, 200 feet: [Male], October 20, 1963, ADG 326.

This is the only record known to me of this species from North Borneo. Smythies (1960:126) lists 11 specimens from other parts of Borneo.

=Egretta sacra= (Gmelin): Reef Egret.--The species was observed at

Karindingen Island on August 17 and November 24, 1962, and was the most common egret on the island. One compact flock of 50 was seen at high tide. No white-phased birds were in the flock.

=Bubulcus ibis coromandus= (Boddaert): Cattle Egret.--Specimen, 1: Tongod: [Female], October 21, 1963, ADG 328.

Individuals were observed daily at Tuaran with cattle at the Agricultural Research Centre. I saw them on December 9 when I arrived at Tuaran and again on January 13, when I departed.

=Ardeola bacchus= (Bonaparte): Chinese Pond Heron.--Specimen, 1: 12 mi. N Kalabakan: [Female], October 26, 1962, MCT 3151.

The specimen was brought to our camp by a local boy who obtained it on a stream that ran through his kampong (village) near our sulap (hut). The stream was a small one that ran out of the primary forest, through the village, and back into secondary forest.

=Butorides striatus= (Linnaeus): Little Green Heron.--Specimens, 2: Telipok: [Female], March 10, 1963, TM 67; Sex?, December 13, 1962, TM 6.

This heron was seen at Karindingen Island on August 17, 1962, in a small swamp near the Tawau airport on September 16, and on the reef at Siamil Island on September 18. The specimens collected at Telipok were not identified to subspecies.

=Ixobrychus cinnamomeus cinnamomeus= (Gmelin): Chestnut Bittern.-- Specimen, 1: Tuaran: Sex?, December 24, 1963, SCFC 32.

This specimen was probably taken in the paddy around the Agricultural Research Centre, where I saw Chestnut Bitterns in January 1963.

=Leptoptilos javanicus= (Horsfield): Lesser Adjutant Stork.--Specimen, 1:

Karindingen Island: [Male] testis small, November 24, 1962, MCT 3311.

My first observation of this species was at Karindingen Island on August 17, when approximately 100 birds were seen feeding on the coral sand and reefs. I saw them also within a mile of Semporna along the ship channel, usually in the vicinity of fish traps. On August 31 two birds flew high overhead at Quoin Hill, proceeding in the direction of Cowie Harbor. On November 24, large numbers at Karindingen Island were sitting in mangroves and feeding on the reefs around the island. Two birds were caught by the rising tide while feeding on the reef and were unable to take off. One of these was shot in approximately six to seven feet of water; its feathers were completely waterlogged. Interestingly the flaky skin of the crown had blue-green algae growing on it. These birds were heard calling many times on the reef and in the mangroves; the call is much like the deep growl of a dog.

Sims, Banks, and Harrison have found the storks common in this area (Smythies, 1957:569). Although I could find no evidence of it, possibly Karindingen Island is a nesting locality.

=Anas querquedula= Linnaeus: Garganey.--Specimen, 1: Kg. Banjar: sex? November 13, 1963, ADG 329.

This teal obtained by Garcia is our only record of any duck from North Borneo.

=Haliastur indus= (Boddaert): Brahminy Kite.--This common resident of the Cocoa Research Station was observed almost daily while I was in the field. It seemed to prefer the cleared areas replanted to cocoa and oil palm and was common also at Tawau, Semporna, and Karindingen Island.

=Accipiter trivirgatus microstictus= Mayr: Crested Goshawk.--Specimens, 2: Pintasan Agriculture Station: [Male], October 17, 1963, ADG 314. Cocoa Research Station: [Male], April 30, 1963, ADG 89.

=Spizaetus cirrhatus limnaetus= (Horsfield): Changeable Hawk-eagle.--Specimen, 1: Tiger Estate: [Male], April 28, 1963, ADG 74 (Specimen in black phase).

=Hieraetus kienerii formosus= (E. Geoffroy): Rufous-bellied Hawk-eagle.--Specimens, 2: Cocoa Research Station: [Female] imm., July 10, 1962, MCT 2615. Tiger Estate: [Female], July 13, 1962, MCT 2621.

The presence of an immature bird of this species in North Borneo lends support to the suggestion of Smythies (1957:580) that this species breeds in Borneo.

fHaliaeetus leucogaster= (Gmelin): White-bellied Sea Eagle.--This eagle appears to be fairly common along the coast in the Tawau-Darvel Bay area. I saw it around Cowie Harbor, Tawau, Semporna, and Siamil Island.

=Spilornis cheela= Latham: Crested Serpent Eagle.--I saw this eagle but once, circling overhead at the Cocoa Research Station on September 26, 1962.

=Microhierax latifrons= Sharpe: White-fronted Falconet.--Specimens, 2: Cocoa Research Station: [Male] testis 2 ?1 mm., 41.2 gm., July 6, 1962, MCT 2600. Tiger Estate: [Female] oviduct regressing, old brood patch, December 1, 1962, MCT 3418.

This species was first seen at the Cocoa Research Station. The specimen taken there bobbed its head in the manner of various other falcons. On two occasions individuals were observed sitting in a low tree in the front yard of a home in Kalabakan.

These records extend the known range of this species south from Darvel Bay (Smythies, 1960:161) to Cowie Harbor.

=Falco peregrinus japonensis= Gmelin: Peregrine Falcon.--Specimen, 1: Kampong Kuamut: [Male], October 20, 1963, ADG 327.

=Coturnix chinensis= (Linnaeus): Painted Quail.--Specimen, 1: Cocoa Research Station: [Male] testis 8 ?5 mm., September 6, 1962, MCT 2881.

This specimen is intermediate between C. c. lineata and C. c. caerulescens, tending slightly toward the latter in having more rufous coloring on the tertials. R. E. Kuntz took a male at Ranau (USNM 472504) that was also intermediate in its characters but was referable to C. c. lineata. These two specimens, when compared with series of specimens from the Philippines and Sumatra, fitted into a clinal progression of increasingly rufous tertials toward Sumatra. Peters (1934:96) united C. c. caerulescens with C. c. palmeri, but Amadon (in litt.) retains C. c. caerulescens (Smythies, 1957:588). No clear-cut distributional pattern is yet discernible in North Borneo and the arrangement of Amadon (MS) should probably be reviewed again when more specimens become available.

These birds were observed several times at the Cocoa Research Station but were difficult to collect. They were abundant in the grasslands on the Brantian Estate.

=Rollulus roulroul= (Scopoli): Crested Green Wood Partridge.--It was observed once along the Apas River at the Cocoa Research Station, in primary forest.

=Haematortyx sanguiniceps= Sharpe: Crimson-headed Wood Partridge.-- Frederick Dunn saw one fly across the padang at the Cocoa Research Station rest house on September 9.

=Lophura ignita= (Shaw and Nodder): Crested Fireback Pheasant.-- Specimens, 3: Cocoa Research Station: [Female], molting, July 20, 1962, MCT 2624. 12 mi. N Kalabakan: [Female], November 4, 1962, MCT 3206; [Male], November 7, 1962, MCT 3216.

This pheasant was taken in native snares from primary forest.

=Lophura bulweri= (Sharpe): Bulwer's Pheasant.--Specimens, 3: 5.5 mi. SW Tenom: [Female], December 25, 1962, MCT 3534; [Male], December 27, 1962, MCT 3539; [Female], December 27, 1962, MCT 3540.

This bird was first taken in a snare 12 miles north of Kalabakan. Unfortunately, the specimen was stolen and only its tail feathers were brought in by the trappers. Mr. Comber of Sapong Estates in Tenom said this species comes in numbers with the wild-pig migration and that he had observed this at least three times. He has also seen three-quarters grown young at Tenom, so they seemingly nest there. They were found only in primary forest.

These specimens constitute the first records of the species for the west coast of North Borneo (cf. Smythies, 1957:593).

=Argusianus argus grayi= (Elliott): Great Argus Pheasant.--Specimens, 6: 12 mi. N Kalabakan: [Male], October 14, 1962, MCT 3034; [Female], October 22, 1962, MCT 3121; [Male], October 23, 1962, MCT 3130; [Male], October 27, 1962, MCT 3166; [Female]?, October 29, 1962, MCT 3307. 5.5 mi. SW Tenom: [Female], December 19, 1962, MCT 3464.

This species is a common resident of the primary forest at Kalabakan and in the lower areas around Tenom (J. A. Comber, pers. comm.). It is found only in primary forest.

=Rallina fasciata= (Raffles): Malaysian Banded Crake.--Specimen, 1: Tiger Estate: [Male], July 11, 1963, ADG 193.

=Amaurornis phoenicurus javanicus= (Horsfield): White-breasted Waterhen.--Specimens, 3: Tuaran: sex?, March 1, 1963, ADG 5. Telipok: [Female], February 2, 1963, TM 23; [Male], February 2, 1963, TM 24.

This species was commonly observed in marshes near Tawau and on the

Brantian Estate.

=Gallicrex cinerea= (Gmelin): Watercock.--Specimen, 1: Tiger Estate: sex?, December 17, 1962 (taken on dry grassland).

=Squatarola squatarola= (Linnaeus): Black-bellied Plover.--On September 2 I saw a flock of 12 plovers on the Tawau golf course. They were in a mottled plumage indicating extensive molt and feather growth. Later in the day a bird in almost complete breeding plumage flew overhead.

=Charadrius peroni= Schlegel: Malay Sand Plover.--On September 15, one was sitting on the Tawau Airport runway. Another was observed on November 20, feeding near a water buffalo wallow on the Brantian Estate. Smythies (1960:191) lists sandy beaches as the only habitat.

=Charadrius leschenaulti= Lesson: Large Sand Plover.--On September 16 one was sitting on the Tawau Airport runway.

=Numenius phaeopus variegatus= (Scopoli): Whimbrel.--Specimen, 1: Karindingen Island: [Male], November 24, 1962, MCT 3315.

This was the most common curlew around Karindingen Island on November 24. Flocks of 10 to 20 individuals were feeding on the coral sand around the island, and a few individuals were sitting in the tops of dead mangroves at low tide.

=Numenius arquata= (Linnaeus): Common Curlew.--On November 24, a Common Curlew flew from Karindingen Island toward the mainland.

=Numenius madagascariensis= (Linnaeus): Eastern Curlew.--I first observed this curlew on August 17 at Karindingen Island, where 50 were feeding on the coral sand. At that time it was the most abundant shorebird. When I returned to the island on November 24, several were seen around the island, but the species was not so abundant as N. phaeopus.

=Limosa lapponica= (Linnaeus): Bar-tailed Godwit.--A flock of five was observed at Karindingen Island on November 24.

=Tringa totanus eurhinus= (Oberholser): Redshank.--Specimens, 2: Karindingen Island: [Female], November 24, 1962, MCT 3312; [Female], November 24, 1962, MCT 3313.

On August 17, this bird was common and feeding on the coral sand at Karindingen Island. When I revisited the island on November 24 the Redshank seemed to prefer the mangrove areas for feeding and was the most common wader.

=Tringa ochropus= Linnaeus: Green Sandpiper.--Specimen, 1: Brantian Estate: [Female], November 19, 1962, MCT 3305.

The specimen, one of three or four birds seen, was taken near a grassland pond.

=Heteroscelus incanum= (Gmelin): Wandering Tattler.--One was feeding along a sandy beach and later on rocks on Siamil Island on September 18, 1962.

=Capella megala= (Swinhoe): Swinhoe's Snipe.--Specimens, 3: Tiger Estate: sex?, December 9, 1962; sex?, December 9, 1962. Pintasan Agriculture Station: [Male], October 17, 1963, ADG 317.

These three specimens lend support to the theory of Smythies (1960:206) that this species is the common snipe of North Borneo.

=Calidris canutus= (Linnaeus): Knot.--On August 17, I saw 20 Knots feeding on the coral sand at Karindingen Island. They were still partly in breeding feather, showing rusty color here and there on the breast. I saw no Knots on November 24 at Karindingen Island. There is but one prior record for Borneo, from the North Natuna Islands (Chasen, 1935:39).

=Erolia ruficollis= (Pallas): Red-necked Stint.--Specimen, 1: Karindingen Island: [Male], November 24, 1962, MCT 3314.

The species was common on November 24 around Karindingen Island, usually in flocks of 5 to 10 birds.

=Glareola pratincola= (Linnaeus): Collared Pratincole.--Specimen, 1: Tiger Estate: [Male], April 28, 1963, ADG 75.

=Chlidonias hybrida= (Pallas): Whiskered Tern.--Specimen, 1: Kuala Sumawang: sex?, September 18, 1962, ADG 280.

Smythies (1960:217) lists no record for North Borneo.

=Sterna bergii= Lichtenstein: Greater Crested Tern.--Specimens, 2: Kuala Sumawang: [Female], September 18, 1963, ADG 278; [Male], September 18, 1963, ADG 279.

This tern was observed several times off the coast of North Borneo near Tawau.

=Treron curvirostra curvirostra= (Gmelin): Thick-billed Pigeon.--Specimens, 9: Cocoa Research Station: [Male] testis 9 ?5 mm., 166.7 gm., August 1, 1962, MCT 2693; [Male] testis 5 ?4 mm., 167.2 gm., August 1, 1962, MCT 2694; [Male] testis 13 ?6 mm., 167.8 gm., August 1, 1962, MCT 2695; [Male] testis 9 ?5 mm., 155.5 gm., August 1, 1962, MCT 2700; [Female], 112.9 gm., August 2, 1962, MCT 2712; [Male], 185.8 gm., August 2, 1962, MCT 2713; [Female], 135.4 gm., growing new 5th primary, August 25, 1962, MCT 2806; [Female], 132.2 gm., August 31, 1962, MCT 2842; [Male], 112.5 gm., August 31, 1962, MCT 2843.

This pigeon was the most common bird eating wild figs (Ficus) in the communal feeding trees, where there were as many as 30 gathered in one tree to feed. While resting, individual birds commonly dipped their tails.

=Treron olax olax= (Temminck): Little Green Pigeon.--Specimens, 2: Cocoa Research Station: [Male] testis 11 ?5 mm., September 1, 1962, MCT 2844. Pintasan Agriculture Station: [Male], October 14, 1963, ADG 306.

The species was seen only once. At the Cocoa Research Station, one bird sat on a dead tree and fed on a red berry from a vine. The call resembled the crying of a child. Others called in the cocoa. The bird taken had testes of a size indicating possible breeding condition.

=Treron vernans purpurea= (Gmelin): Pink-necked Green Pigeon.-- Specimens, 10: Tiger Estate: [Male], November 25, 1962, MCT 3323; [Female], November 25, 1962, MCT 3325. Telipok: [Female], January 31, 1963, TM 22; [Female], January 31, 1963, TM 20; [Male], January 31, 1963, TM 19; [Female], January 31, 1963, TM 21; [Male], February 10, 1963, TM 35; [Male], February 2, 1963, TM 25. Mt. Rumas: [Female], March 6, 1963, ADG 11. Tuaran: [Female], November 29, 1963, SCFC 34.

The species was confined to the lowlands around Tawau, as at the Tawau Airport in the scrub growth. Flocks of 50 to 100 were observed at Tuaran. None of the specimens taken in November was in breeding condition.

=Ducula bicolor= (Scopoli): Pied Imperial Pigeon.--I observed this pigeon on September 18 and 19 at Siamil Island. On the first day two were seen in the few remaining trees on the island and on September 19 a flock of 12 flew southwest over the island at about 8:30 A. M.

=Streptopelia bitorquata= (Temminck): Javanese Turtle Dove.--On Siamil Island on September 18 and 19, two were seen at close range feeding with 10 S. chinensis. There is only one other record from Borneo; Pryer took one at Sandakan in the 1880's (Everett, 1889:193) and it has not been recorded since. Chasen (1935:22) speculated that the Javanese Turtle Dove was introduced to Borneo as a cage bird. But, Borneo is seemingly well within the normal range of the species and probably it is a resident of North Borneo. The Javanese Turtle Dove and the Spotted-necked Dove, S. chinensis, closely resemble each other; this resemblance may help to account for the lack of records of S. bitorquata.

=Streptopelia chinensis= (Scopoli): Spotted-necked Dove.--Specimens, 2: Tiger Estate: [Male], June 19, 1963, ADG 149. Telipok: [Male], February 10, 1963, TM 34.

This is a common bird of the coconut groves around Tawau and on Siamil Island.

=Chalcophaps indica= (Linnaeus): Emerald Dove.--Specimen, 1: Cocoa Research Station: [Male], June 17, 1963, ADG 146.

Birds, always solitary, of this species often were seen in the cocoa groves at the Cocoa Research Station.

=Tanygnathus lucionensis lucionensis= (Linnaeus): Blue-naped Parrot.--Specimens, 3: Siamil Island: [Male], September 19, 1962, MCT 2928; [Female], September 19, 1962, MCT 2929; [Female], September 19, 1962, MCT 2930.

These birds were seen on September 18 and 19. I saw flocks of 10 to 20 in the remnant of forest on the north side of the island. The birds were almost entirely inhabitants of the forest and were rarely seen in the coconut groves. I estimated the entire island population to be between 30 and 100 birds. The Japanese residents knew nothing of the birds, although they were aware of a cockatoo (Cacatua galerita) that had lived at large on the island for several years. The Blue-naped Parrot has been found only on the Maratuas and on Mantanani Island. Smythies (1960:242) surmised that the Mantanani population was introduced by sailing craft from the Sulu Sea. In the light of the present discovery, I think the species is a naturally-established resident of the North Bornean islands.

=Psittinus cyanurus cyanurus= (Forester): Little Malay Parrot.--Specimens, 2: Tiger Estate: [Female], October 11, 1962, MCT 2998; [Male], October 11, 1962, MCT 2997.

Smythies (1963:277) was the first to record this species from North Borneo. However, the Harvard Primate Expedition in 1938 took three specimens as follows: [Male], Sandakan, June 6, 1937, MCZ 197123; [Male], Morutai Besar, June 27, 1937, MCZ 197124; [Male], Kalabakan River, July 16, 1937, MCZ 197125. The Harvard collection of birds from North Borneo appears to have been overlooked, although it was mentioned in passing by Smythies (1960:526). The specimens in my collection were taken in the same general area where H. G. Deignan took the Harvard specimens.

=Loriculus galgulus= (Linnaeus): Malay Lorikeet.--Specimen, 1: Cocoa Research Station: [Female], May 1, 1963, ADG 103.

This lorikeet was rare at all of our collecting localities.

=Cuculus fugax fugax= Horsfield: Malayan Hawk-Cuckoo.--Specimens, 3: Cocoa Research Station: [Male], 86.0 gm., August 28, 1963, MCT 2825; [Male], 79.0 gm., September 11, 1962, MCT 2899; [Female], September 28, 1962, MCT 2977.

This species was first observed on August 28 in primary forest and was seen regularly from then until September 28 in secondary forest, primary forest, and in cocoa shade trees.

=Cacomantis sonnerati= (Latham): Banded Bay Cuckoo.--Birds that may have been of this species were observed on several occasions. E. J. H. Berwick (pers. comm.) claimed he had heard C. sonnerati at the Cocoa Research Station. I have heard many times a call sometimes ascribed to this species but I have not actually seen the bird making the sound. If the call note I heard is actually of this species it is not rare in the Quoin Hill area.

=Cacomantis merulinus threnodes= Cabanis and Heine: Plaintive Cuckoo.--
Specimens, 5: Cocoa Research Station: [Male], 25.0 gm., September 8, 1962,
MCT 2891; [Female] imm., 27.0 gm., September 8, 1962, MCT 2892; [Male]
testis 4 ?3 mm., November 29, 1962, MCT 3382. Tenom: [Male], January 1,
1963, MCT 3563. Ulu Balung: [Female], July 15, 1963, ADG 199.

This cuckoo was common in all habitats examined at all of our collecting
stations, except the moss forest near Tenom.

=Cacomantis variolosus sepulchralis= (S. Muller): Fantailed Cuckoo.--
Specimens, 2: Cocoa Research Station: [Male], 30.8 gm., August 28, 1962,
MCT 2824. Ulu Balung: [Male], July 10, 1963, ADG 183.

The specimens were collected in primary forest. There are only five earlier
records for all of Borneo (Smythies, 1960:253-254). Probably this species
nests in Borneo; it is unlikely that specimens taken in August and July are
migrants.

=Chalcites xanthorhynchus xanthorhynchus= (Horsfield): Violet Cuckoo.--
Specimens, 1: Cocoa Research Station: [Female] largest ovum 1 mm.,
September 26, 1962, MCT 2964.

This species was seen twice, both times in the research station cocoa
plantings. The specimen taken was from a shade tree, Trema orientalis.

=Chalcites malayanus aheneus= Junge: Malaysian Green Cuckoo.--
Specimens, 9: Cocoa Research Station: [Female] definite brood patch, 17.5
gm., body molt, July 4, 1962, MCT 2587; [Male] testis 4 ?4 mm., 19.1 gm.,
August 8, 1962, MCT 2736; [Female], 17.5 gm., August 8, 1962, MCT 2737;
[Male], 17.5 gm., August 8, 1962, MCT 2738; [Male] testis 4 ?3 mm., 18.2 gm.,
August 8, 1962, MCT 2739; [Female], August 25, 1962, MCT 2809; [Male],
21.1 gm., September 11, 1962, MCT 2900; [Male], October 2, 1962, MCT 2984.
Tiger Estate: [Female] oviduct enlarged, brood patch, November 25, 1962,

MCT 3318.

This cuckoo was common in the cocoa planting at the Cocoa Research Station and not found in any other type of habitat. Smythies (1960:255) thought that possibly two species of Chalcites were represented in the series of Chalcites malayanus from Borneo. I have assembled all 20 known specimens, however, including seven in the Museum of Comparative Zoology at Harvard unreported by Smythies (1957:638) and find that the variation in the coloration of the head and upperparts is due to the difference in sexes, the males being darker than the females. There is much variation in the length of the wing, but the meaning of this variation is not yet clear.

=Surniculus lugubris barussarum= (Oberholser): Drongo-cuckoo.--Specimens, 2: Cocoa Research Station: [Female] imm., July 28, 1962, MCT 2672, discarded; [Female] imm., 28.6 gm., August 25, 1962, MCT 2810.

The first specimen was taken in secondary forest; it had been sitting in a dead tree, occasionally darting out after insects. The second specimen was taken in cocoa; its stomach contained 50 caterpillars.

=Eudynamys scolopacea= (Linnaeus): Koel.--This species was observed at Tawau and on Siamil Island, on August 30 and September 18, respectively.

=Clamator coromandus= (Linnaeus): Red-winged Crested Cuckoo.--Specimen, 1: Telipok: [Female], February 10, 1963, TM 33.

=Phaenicophaeus chlorophaeus fuscigularis= (Baker): Raffles Malcoha.-- Specimen, 1: Cocoa Research Station: [Male], August 26, 1962, MCT 2813.

Flocks of three and four were seen in the cocoa. At Kalabakan the species was feeding about 40 feet up in the second canopy layer of the primary forest.

=Phaenicophaeus diardi borneensis= (Salvadori): Lesser Green-billed Malcoha.--Specimens, 3: Cocoa Research Station: [Female], 58.2 gm., July 22,

1962, MCT 2636; [Female], 55.8 gm., September 8, 1962, MCT 2890; [Male], September 13, 1962, MCT 2918.

This malcoha was seen only three times; it was the second most common malcoha.

=Phaenicophaeus javanicus pallidus= (Robinson and Kloss): Red-billed Malcoha.--Specimens, 2: Cocoa Research Station: [Female], 97.0 gm., August 31, 1962, MCT 2841; [Male], 98.0 gm., September 8, 1962, MCT 2889.

The two specimens were taken in cocoa. On October 2, 1962, I saw one about 100 feet up in the top canopy layer of the primary forest at the Cocoa Research Station and, on October 3, two more hopping from branch to branch about 150 feet up in a tree.

=Phaenicophaeus curvirostris borneensis= (Blasius and Nehrkorn): Chestnut-breasted Malcoha.--Specimens, 7: Cocoa Research Station: [Female] old brood patch, 121.8 gm., July 6, 1962, MCT 2602; [Female], September 4, 1962, MCT 2864; [Male] testis 3 ?2 mm., 143.6 gm., wing molt, July 7, 1962, MCT 2611; [Male] testis 6 ?2 mm., 111.0 gm., August 11, 1962, MCT 2763; [Female], May 25, 1963, ADG 110. Ulu Balung: sex?, July 24, 1963, ADG 216. Tiger Estate: [Male], June 22, 1963, ADG 156.

This was the most numerous of the malcohas at the Cocoa Research Station. It was observed in primary forest, secondary forest, citrus trees, and cocoa trees. In the primary forest it ranged in the upper canopy from 100 to 150 feet up.

As Peters has indicated (1940:56), the name P. c. borneensis (Blasius and Nehrkorn) 1881 has priority over P. c. microrhinus Berlepsch 1895 (used by Smythies).

=Centropus sinensis= (Stephens): Common Coucal.--Specimen, 1: Cocoa Research Station: [Female], May 15, 1963, ADG 108.

The finding of a coucal at the Cocoa Research Station on May 15, 1963, came as something of a surprise, since none had been seen there earlier by our group. Coucals were seen at Tawau but were not collected or identified to species.

=Centropus bengalensis= (Gmelin): Lesser Coucal.--Specimens, 2: Tuaran: [Female], April 1, 1963, ADG 46; sex?, December 3, 1963, SCFC 17.

=Carpococcyx radiceus radiceus= (Temminck): Ground Cuckoo.--Specimen, 1: 12 mi. N Kalabakan: [Male] imm., November 7, 1962, MCT 3217.

This male was taken in a native snare in primary forest and provides our only record. The specimen is in the postjuvenal (first prebasic) molt.

This record is the first for this species from North Borneo (Smythies, 1957:643); others are known from Sarawak and Indonesian Borneo.

=Otus bakkamoena lemurum= Deignan. Collared Scops Owl.--Specimens, 3: Tiger Estate: [Female], November 25, 1962, MCT 3319. Tenom: [Male] testis 6 ?5 mm., body molt, January 1, 1963, MCT 3552. Agricultural Oil Palm Station: [Male], October 6, 1963, ADG 299.

The specimen from Tenom was taken in a bird net set in a grass-scrubland situation; the testes were regressing. Harrison (Smythies, 1957:645) found this species breeding in the Kelabit uplands in January.

=Glaucidium brodiei borneense= Sharpe: Pygmy Owlet.--Specimen, 1: Ulu Balung: [Male], July 19, 1963, ADG 210.

The specimen taken by Garcia is the sixth known (Smythies, 1957:646) from Borneo and the first from the east coast. Specimens were collected in 1956 in North Borneo by the Cambridge Expedition.

=Ninox scutulata borneensis= (Bonaparte): Hawk-owl.--Specimen, 1: Tenom: [Female] largest ovum 2 mm., oviduct evident, January 6, 1963, MCT 3583.

This female, taken in a bird net in a grass-scrubland association, was coming into breeding condition.

=Strix leptogrammica= Temminck: Malaysian Wood Owl.--Specimens, 2: Cocoa Research Station: sex?, July 9, 1963, ADG 182; [Male], May 25, 1963, ADG 111.

On September 7, 1962, I flushed two of these owls from a tree beside the Apas River in primary forest. One was subsequently shot but lost. Garcia's two specimens were not identified to subspecies.

=Caprimulgus macrurus salvadori= Sharpe: Long-tailed Nightjar.--Specimens, 3: Tuaran: [Female], January 12, 1963, MCT 3592; [Female], March 2, 1963, ADG 6. Mt. Rumas: [Male], March 6, 1963, ADG 13.

This was an abundant bird on the Jesselton-Tuaran road but was not seen at any of the other collecting stations in North Borneo.

=Collocalia fuciphaga natunae= Stresemann: Thunberg Swiftlet.--Specimens, 3: Cocoa Research Station: [Female] largest ovum 7 mm., oviduct enlarged, 13.1 gm., June 30, 1962, MCT 2570; [Female] ovary small, September 8, 1962, MCT 2887. 5.5 mi. SW Tenom: [Female], December 20, 1962, MCT 3485.

This swiftlet was seen every day while we were at the Cocoa Research Station and was common also in the mountains around Tenom, where it flew in and out of the fog over our camp.

=Collocalia esculenta= ssp.: White-bellied Swiftlet.--Specimens, 7: Cocoa Research Station: [Male], 5.5 gm., July 4, 1962, MCT 2591; [Male], 6.2 gm., July 5, 1962, MCT 2594; [Male], 6.2 gm., July 1, 1962, MCT 2574; [Female], 6.0 gm., July 4, 1962, MCT 2589; [Female], 5.7 gm., July 4, 1962, MCT 2590. 12 mi.

N Kalabakan: [Male] testis 4 ?2 mm., November 10, 1962, MCT 3236; [Male], November 10, 1962, MCT 3237.

This was the most abundant of all the swifts at the Cocoa Research Station and in the Kalabakan area and was seen also at Semporna on August 16, 1962, in a small coral cave near the District Officer's house. This cave was 10 feet high at most, but averaged five to six feet. It harbored about 1,000 birds, most of them nesting back in the dimly lit zone but one small group of 50 nested in the entrance in bright light. The adults were still feeding young, although the latter could fly strongly.

=Chaetura leucopygialis= (Blyth): White-rumped Spine-tailed Swift.-- Specimens, 12: Cocoa Research Station: [Female] well-developed brood patch, June 28, 1962, MCT 2565; [Female], 12.9 gm., June 30, 1962, MCT 2567; [Female], June 30, 1962, heavy molt on body, head, wing, tail, MCT 2568; [Female], 14.5 gm., June 30, 1962, MCT 2569; [Female], 13.0 gm., June 30, 1962, MCT 2571; [Female], 13.0 gm., July 1, 1962, MCT 2572; [Male] testis 4 ?2 mm., 12.3 gm., July 1, 1962, MCT 2575; [Male] testis 2 ?1 mm., 14.9 gm., July 2, 1962, MCT 2576; [Female], 15.4 gm., July 5, 1962, MCT 2595; [Male] testis 2 ?1 mm., 15.4 gm., wing molt, July 5, 1962, MCT 2596; [Male] testis 2 ?1 mm., 11.9 gm., July 6, 1962, MCT 2598; [Female], 13.0 gm., July 6, 1962, MCT 2599.

This species was common around the Cocoa Research Station but was not seen elsewhere. There is some variation in color within the populations.

=Hemiprocne comata comata= (Temminck): White-whiskered Tree Swift.-- Specimens, 3: Cocoa Research Station: [Male] testis 2 ?1 mm., 17.0 gm., July 28, 1962, MCT 2675; sex?, young in juvenal plumage, MCT 2812; [Male], April 28, 1963, ADG 76.

At the Cocoa Research Station this common bird usually was seen sitting on a dead branch of a shade tree in the cocoa whence it would dart out after insects. It rarely perched higher than 12 feet. Occasionally it was seen in a clearing in the primary forest.

=Hemiprocne longipennis longipennis= (Rafinesque): Crested Tree Swift.--Specimens, 2: Cocoa Research Station: [Male] testis 4 ?3 mm., September 4, 1962, MCT 2866; sex?, 42.8 gm., September 8, 1962, MCT 2888.

These swifts also were common at the Cocoa Research Station. Unlike H. comata, these birds flew high and sat far up in trees while resting. I never observed them in the primary forest.

The two specimens were more greenish-blue dorsally than typical H. l. longipennis. Specimens from Java were paler gray ventrally and their tertials were more nearly white. Too few specimens were available to permit determination of the constancy of the mentioned variation and the two from the station are referred to the nominate subspecies until more material becomes available.

=Harpactes diardi diardi= (Temminck): Diard's Trogon.--Specimens, 8: Cocoa Research Station: [Female], 95.9 gm., July 2, 1962, MCT 2579; 3 alcoholic naked young, July 3, 1962, presumed young of 2579, MCT 2581-83; [Female], 95.0 gm., August 20, 1962, MCT 2782; [Male] testis 6 ?3 mm., September 5, 1962, MCT 2870; [Male], September 5, 1962, MCT 2871; [Male], December 1, 1962, MCT 3409.

This was the most numerous of the trogons at the Cocoa Research Station. One female was taken in a live trap set for rats in the cocoa. The next day a laborer found a young, presumably of that female, in a nest in the same area. On August 20, a flock of 5 to 10 birds was seen moving together in a loose group through the jungle. This species appeared to be a bird of the primary forest, but occasionally was found in the cocoa.

=Harpactes kasumba impavidus= (Chasen and Kloss): Red-naped Trogon.--Specimens, 2: Cocoa Research Station: [Male], 72.1 gm., August 5, 1962, MCT 3730 (discarded); [Female], September 7, 1962, MCT 2883.

This species of the deep forest was not seen in any other habitat.

=Harpactes duvauceli= (Temminck): Scarlet-rumped Trogon.--Specimens, 7: Cocoa Research Station: [Female], 30.9 gm., July 24, 1962, MCT 2648; [Male]?, December 1, 1962, MCT 3407; [Male], December 1, 1962, MCT 3408. Ulu Balung: [Female], July 18, 1963, ADG 209; [Male], July 18, 1963, ADG 208. Kinabatangan Agricultural Station: [Female], October 13, 1963, ADG 305. 12 mi. N Kalabakan: [Female], October 10, 1962, MCT 2996.

This trogon of the primary forest was second in abundance only to H. diardi.

=Halcyon concreta= (Temminck): Chestnut-collared Kingfisher.--Specimens, 2: 12 mi. N Kalabakan: [Male], November 8, 1962, MCT 3222; [Female], November 8, 1962, MCT 3223.

This kingfisher was netted near a small stream in the deep primary forest. Another individual was obtained in moss forest at an elevation of 4,000 feet at Tenom, but was discarded.

=Halcyon chloris chloroptera= (Oberholser): White-collared Kingfisher.-- Specimens, 4: 9.5 mi. E Tawau: [Female] largest ovum 3 mm., 61.7 gm., July 29, 1962, MCT 2683; [Male] testis 5 ?4 mm., 60.3 gm., July 29, 1962, paired with 2683. Telipok: [Female], February 9, 1963, G. R. Conway; [Female], February 10, 1963, G. R. Conway.

This is a bird of the sea coast. It was seen at Tawau, Siamil Island, and Karindingen Island.

=Halcyon sancta sancta= (Vigors and Horsfield): Sacred Kingfisher.-- Specimen, 1: Cocoa Research Station: [Male], June 17, 1963, ADG 147.

The specimen was taken along the Apas River in scrubland near the river. One previously was recorded from North Borneo, this from Labuan (Smythies,

1957:660). He (1963:278) saw another at Bauto on the Labuk River.

=Halcyon pileata= (Boddaert): Black-capped Kingfisher.--Specimens, 3: Tenom: [Male], January 1, 1963, MCT 3564. Pintasan Agriculture Station: [Female], October 18, 1963, ADG 322; [Male], October 11, 1963, ADG 301.

The specimen from Tenom was caught in a net in the scrub-grassland association. The others were taken along the Kinabatangan River.

=Pelargopsis capensis fraseri= Sharpe: Stork-billed Kingfisher.--Specimens, 2: Telipok: [Male], February 9, 1963, TM 30. Mt. Rumas: [Male], April 16, 1963, ADG 53.

This species was common along the lower reaches of the Kalabakan and Brantian rivers and in the mangroves near Tawau.

=Alcedo atthis bengalensis= Gmelin: Common Kingfisher.--Specimen, 1: Pintasan Agriculture Station: [Female], October 12, 1963, ADG 304.

I saw this kingfisher once along the Apas River at Quoin Hill and again along the beach at Siamil Island.

=Alcedo euryzona euryzona= Temminck: Blue-banded Kingfisher.-- Specimens, 4: Cocoa Research Station: [Male], September 7, 1962, MCT 2884. 12 mi. N Kalabakan: [Male], October 19, 1962, MCT 3091; [Female], October 20, 1962, MCT 3099; [Male], October 20, 1962, MCT 3101.

This species was fairly common along streams deep in the primary forest at Quoin Hill.

=Ceyx erithacus= ssp. (Linnaeus): Forest Kingfisher.--Specimens, 4: Cocoa Research Station: [Male], 13.2 gm., September 14, 1962, MCT 2924; 12 mi. N Kalabakan: [Male], October 18, 1962, MCT 3075; [Female], October 26, 1962, MCT 3163. Oil Palm Research Station: [Male], September 5, 1963, ADG 273.

All specimens taken showed characters intermediate between those of the subspecies C. e. motleyi and C. e. rufidorsus. Voous (1951) states that, in all the Malaysian region, the greatest number of hybrids between these two subspecies occurred in Borneo and, further, that he could find hybrid specimens showing practically all imaginable character combinations. My specimens also showed these intermediate tendencies and I am unable at present to allocate the specimens to subspecies.

=Merops viridis viridis= Linnaeus: Blue-throated Bee-eater.--Specimens, 9: Mt. Rumas: [Male], March 5, 1963, ADG 9; [Male], March 5, 1963, ADG 10; [Female], March 6, 1963, ADG 20; [Male], March 7, 1963, ADG 21; [Female], March 7, 1963, ADG 22; [Male], March 7, 1963, ADG 23. Telipok: [Female], March 24, 1963; ADG 39. Pintasan: [Male], October 22, 1963, ADG 302; [Female], October 12, 1963, ADG 303.

These specimens were all taken in March and October and seem to support Smythies' (1957:664) idea that they arrive with the northeast monsoon (October to March) and are absent the rest of the year.

=Nyctiornis amicta= (Temminck): Red-bearded Bee-eater.--Specimen, 1: Cocoa Research Station: [Male], September 27, 1962, molting, MCT 2970.

The specimen was taken along a stream in the deep primary forest, where it was sitting on a dead twig overlooking the stream. The call note was much like that of a scolding squirrel. This was the only time this species was observed in the Quoin Hill area.

=Eurystomus orientalis cyanicollis= Vieillot: Broad-billed Roller.--Specimens, 4: Cocoa Research Station: [Male] testis 2 ?1 mm., 157.4 gm., heavy molt, July 3, 1962, MCT 2585; [Male] testis 2 ?1 mm., 152.0 gm., heavy molt, July 21, 1962, MCT 2633; [Female], 146.4 gm., heavy molt, July 21, 1962, MCT 2634; [Female], April 29, 1963, ADG 83.

At the Cocoa Research Station this common bird perched in dead trees in the cocoa. On several evenings in September, an individual was seen catching insects in flight at dusk, repeatedly returning to a stump between forays. This continued until it was so dark that I could barely discern the bird.

=Berenicornis comatus= (Raffles): White-crested Hornbill.--A pair was seen feeding about 150 feet up in a tree at the Cocoa Research Station. No other was seen in northern Borneo.

=Annorrhinus galeritus= (Temminck): Bushy-crested Hornbill.--This hornbill was seen only on October 3, 1962, at the Cocoa Research Station, when a flock of five flew overhead.

=Aceros leucocephalus= (Vieillot): Wrinkled Hornbill.--On October 3, 1962, a pair was seen in the primary forest at the Cocoa Research Station.

=Aceros undulatus undulatus= (Shaw): Wreathed Hornbill.--Specimens, 2: Cocoa Research Station: [Female] largest ovum 5 mm., October 2, 1962, MCT 2981; [Male] testis 10 ?11 mm., October 2, 1962, MCT 2982.

This, the most common hornbill at Quoin Hill and at Kalabakan, occurred in primary forest.

=Anthracoceros malayanus= (Raffles): Black Hornbill.--A flock of five was seen at the Cocoa Research Station rest house on September 6 and 13, 1962.

=Buceros rhinoceros= Linnaeus: Rhinoceros Hornbill.--It was fairly common at the Cocoa Research Station, where several were observed in July and August.

=Rhinoplax vigil= (Forster): Helmeted Hornbill.--The Helmeted Hornbill was rarely observed, but almost every day we heard its call when we were on the east coast. It was also heard in the forest on the west coast around Tenom, but is not common there owing to hunting by the natives. Skulls of this and the preceding species were on sale in a shop at Tenom, despite laws prohibiting the killing of these species.

=Calorhamphus fuliginosus tertius= Chasen and Kloss: Brown Barbet.-- Specimens, 7: Cocoa Research Station: [Female] largest ovum 2 mm., 38.8 gm., brood patch, July 7, 1962, MCT 2610; [Female], 40.0 gm., August 1, 1962, MCT 2702; [Female], 44.8 gm., August 1, 1962, MCT 2703; [Male] testis 5 ?3 mm., September 25, 1962 (paired with MCT 2956), MCT 2955; [Female], September 1, 1962, MCT 2846, [Female], September 25, 1962, MCT 2956; [Female]?, November 30, 1962, MCT 3436.

These barbets were common at the Cocoa Research Station both in secondary forest and cocoa, usually in groups of three or four. They were seen also at Kalabakan where the birds fed in the top of a 100-foot tree in the primary forest.

In describing this bird, Smythies (1960:322) said the male's bill is black. The one male that I took had an orange bill and at no time did I observe any black-billed birds at the Cocoa Research Station; this black bill perhaps is a character of the subspecies C. f. fuliginosus.

=Megalaima henrici brachyrhyncha= Neumann: Yellow-crowned Barbet.-- Specimens, 3: Cocoa Research Station: [Female], 72.8 gm., August 1, 1962, MCT 2696; [Male] testis 5 ?4 mm., 83.2 gm., August 2, 1962, MCT 2705; [Male] testis 6 ?5 mm., 73.7 gm., August 2, 1962, MCT 2706.

This barbet was common at the Cocoa Research Station and its call could be heard at any time of day until dusk. Smythies (1960:324) described this call as took-took-took-took-trrrroook. All birds of this species that I watched and listened to, however, were calling thus: trrrroook-took-took-took-took. The number of tooks varies, but is generally four and can be as high as seven. This species was heard at all stations on the east coast. At Kalabakan, one was heard calling all day long from the top of a 70-foot tree.

Comparison of my specimens with those in the U. S. National Museum revealed that M. h. brachyrhyncha was readily distinguishable from the nominate race by measurements. The average length of bill in my specimens was 23 mm., whereas the average length in two specimens from Sumatra and Siam in the U. S. National Museum was 27 mm. The Bornean specimens differ also in having the blue patch on the head larger and darker than in M. h. henrici. M. h. brachyrhyncha certainly seems to be a valid race on the basis of the available specimens.

=Megalaima chrysopogon chrysopsis= Goffin: Gold-whiskered Barbet.-- Specimens, 10: Cocoa Research Station: [Female] largest ovum 2 mm., 164.4 gm., July 21, 1962, MCT 2627; [Male] testis 6 ?3 mm., 156.0 gm., August 1, 1962, MCT 2697; [Female], 177.2 gm., August 1, 1962, MCT 2701; [Male] testis 3 ?2 mm., 172.6 gm., August 2, 1962, MCT 2717; ?, 182.2 gm., August 2, 1962, MCT 2718; [Female], 181.5 gm., MCT 2721; [Male] testis 10 ?8 mm., 148.5 gm., August 8, 1962, MCT 2741; [Male], June 23, 1963, ADG 155; [Female], May 25, 1963, ADG 109. Tiger Estate: [Male], November 25, 1962, MCT 3324.

Next to the Brown Barbet, this was perhaps the most common barbet at the Cocoa Research Station and was often the only bird heard in the heat of the day. On three occasions birds were observed clinging to the side of a tree as a woodpecker might, pecking away at dead wood. This species was seen both in the cocoa and primary forest.

=Megalaima mystacophanes mystacophanes= (Temminck): Gaudy Barbet.-- Specimens, 8: Cocoa Research Station: [Female], 60.3 gm., July 25, 1962; [Male] testis 8 ?5 mm., 79.2 gm., August 9, 1962, MCT 2749; [Male] testis 9 ?5 mm., September 1, 1962, MCT 2845; [Female], September 25, 1962, MCT 2950; [Female], April 30, 1963, ADG 88. 12 mi. N Kalabakan: [Male], October 20, 1962, MCT 3103. 5.5 mi. SW Tenom: [Male] testis 8 ?6 mm., December 25, 1962, MCT 3530; [Female], December 25, 1962, MCT 3537.

This common bird lived in the secondary and primary forest and cocoa. I saw it at all localities. At least two calls were given by this species. One was a simple took with a long pause between calls; the other was as described by Smythies (1960:323).

The birds fed from high in trees down to nearly ground level. This species like M. chrysopogon, clung to the sides of trees and pecked at dead wood.

=Megalaima australis duvauceli= (Lesson): Little Barbet.--Specimens, 3: Cocoa Research Station: [Male] testis 7 ?5 mm., 35.2 gm., August 1, 1962, MCT 2692; [Male] testis 9 ?5 mm., August 1, 1962, MCT 2699; [Female] ovary granular, 33.0 gm., August 1, 1962, MCT 2704.

I was unable to make detailed observations on this species. All specimens were taken from a high feeding tree, where it was impossible to identify them before hand.

=Indicator archipelagicus= Temminck: Malaysian Honey-guide.--Specimens, 2: Cocoa Research Station: [Female] ovary minute, 29 November 1962, MCT 3394. Tenom: [Male] testis 3 ?2 mm., January 5, 1963, MCT 3580.

The specimen from the Cocoa Research Station was taken in a net in the cocoa and the Tenom bird was taken in a net in the middle of Tenom, both in garden areas. These two specimens differ in coloration from Bornean birds in the U. S. National Museum; I think the difference results from "foxing" of the older specimens. Specimens have been taken previously in North Borneo on the Bengkoka River, Lumbidan, and on the Mengalong River (Smythies, 1957:669). Mary Norman saw this honey-guide once at the Quoin Estate in 1962 (Smythies, 1963:279).

=Sasia abnormis= (Temminck): Rufous Piculet.--Specimens, 13: Cocoa Research Station: [Male] testis 3 ?2 mm., molting, July 10, 1962, MCT 2612; [Female], September 24, 1962, MCT 2940; [Female], December 1, 1962, MCT 3411; [Male], July 9, 1963, ADG 177; [Male], July 7, 1963, ADG 166; [Male], June 14, 1963, ADG 135. 12 mi. N Kalabakan: [Female], October 17, 1962,

MCT 3061. 5.5 mi. SW Tenom: [Male], December 19, 1962, MCT 3470; [Female], December 23, 1962, MCT 3517; [Male], December 24, 1962, MCT 3529; [Female], December 27, 1962, MCT 3541. Oil Palm Research Station: [Female], August 24, 1963, ADG 257; [Male], August 15, 1963, ADG 242.

The piculet was common in the secondary undergrowth near the Cocoa Research Station, and was taken once in the primary forest. One bird was seen sitting on a small branch about 10 feet up at a right angle to the branch. It did not ascend the tree like a woodpecker. This species was also taken in the moss forest near Tenom.

=Picus puniceus observandus= (Hartert): Crimson-winged Woodpecker.-- Specimens, 2: Cocoa Research Station: [Female], 65.8 gm., July 27, 1962, MCT 2671; [Male], September 27, 1962, MCT 2973.

This woodpecker was observed twice, both times in primary forest at the Cocoa Research Station.

=Picus mentalis humei= (Hargitt): Checkered-throated Woodpecker.-- Specimens, 2: Cocoa Research Station: [Female], 93.3 gm., July 23, 1962, MCT 2642; sex?, 107.0 gm., August 5, 1962, MCT 2733.

I saw this bird only twice, in primary forest.

=Picus miniaceus malaccensis= Latham: Banded Red Woodpecker.-- Specimen, 1: Cocoa Research Station: [Male] testis 8 ?5 mm., 79.5 gm., August 4, 1962, MCT 2722.

On August 4 I saw two birds of this species together in badly disturbed primary forest and took the specimen listed above.

=Micropternus brachyurus badiosus= (Bonaparte): Rufous Woodpecker.-- Specimens, 5: Cocoa Research Station: [Female] brood patch, 4 to 5 old collapsed follicles, 73.2 gm., July 3, 1962, MCT 2584; [Female], 65.4 gm., July

25, 1962, MCT 2658; [Male] testis 2 ?1 mm., 66.7 gm., July 25, 1962, MCT 2659. Tiger Estate: [Male], June 23, 1963, ADG 158; [Female], June 23, 1963, ADG 159.

I saw this woodpecker but twice, both times at the Cocoa Research Station. A female taken from a dead tree in the cocoa may have been just finishing nesting activities, judging from the size of the ova. A pair seen feeding on the ground near a brush pile in secondary forest was collected. The stomachs contained ants.

=Dendrocopos canicapillus aurantiiventris= (Salvadori): Oriental Pygmy Woodpecker.--Specimens, 2: Cocoa Research Station: sex?, July 22, 1962, MCT 2635; [Male] testis 3 ?2 mm., 23.5 gm., molting, August 25, 1962, MCT 2807.

On July 22 four individuals were feeding on dead trees in the cocoa. They made a cheep cheep sound, rattling calls, and drummed. On August 25, 1962, two were feeding in dead trees in the cocoa. The testes of specimen MCT 2807 were probably regressing since it was beginning the molt.

=Meiglyptes tristis micropternus= Hesse: Fulvous-rumped Barred Woodpecker.--Specimens, 2: Cocoa Research Station: [Female], 31.7 gm., July 7, 1962, MCT 2607; [Male], May 28, 1963, ADG 115.

Compared with M. tukki, this species was comparatively rare. I saw two on July 7 working in a living tree some 15 feet above the ground. The tree was only 20 feet high and had dense foliage. The birds gave a rattling call note of about two seconds duration; it sounded like a typical woodpecker call. The single call note can be rendered cheet. They were also heard drumming, but only softly. The stomachs contained ants, which probably are what the two woodpeckers were feeding on in the green tree.

=Meiglyptes tukki tukki= (Lesson): Buff-necked Barred Woodpecker.-- Specimens, 13: Cocoa Research Station: [Male] testis 2 ?1 mm., heavy molt,

July 10, 1962, MCT 2614; [Female], 53.3 gm., July 28, 1962, MCT 2677; [Male], 51.5 gm., July 28, 1962, MCT 2679; [Female], 48.7 gm., July 28, 1962, MCT 2678; [Male], December 2, 1962, MCT 3423; [Female], December 2, 1962, MCT 3424; [Female], December 2, 1962, MCT 3425. 12 mi. N Kalabakan: [Female], October 26, 1962, MCT 3153. Telipok: [Female], March 24, 1962, ADG 37. Agriculture Oil Palm Research Station: [Female], October 4, 1963, ADG 292; [Female], August 15, 1963, ADG 238; [Female], August 14, 1963, ADG 234. Pintasan Agriculture Station: [Female], October 17, 1963, ADG 313.

This was the most common woodpecker at the Cocoa Research Station. A flock of four was seen on July 28, 1962, and on December 2, 1962, I took three simultaneously in one mist net. The species has flocking tendencies. Calls heard were a typical woodpecker rattle.

=Dinopium rafflesi dulitense= Delacour: Olive-backed Three-toed Woodpecker.--Specimens, 4: Cocoa Research Station: [Male] testis 11 ?7 mm., July 12, 1962, MCT 2620; [Male], September 6, 1962, MCT 2879. 12 mi. N Kalabakan: [Male], October 20, 1962, MCT 3097. Oil Palm Research Station: [Male], August 12, 1963, ADG 227.

The species was taken in both primary and secondary forest. The specimen collected at the Cocoa Research Station on July 12 suggests that the species breeds there.

=Dryocopus javensis javensis= (Horsfield): Great Black Woodpecker.--Specimens, 4: Cocoa Research Station: [Female] old brood patch, 284.7 gm., light body and tail molt, July 6, 1962, MCT 2601; [Male] by plumage, July 19, 1962, MCT 2625; [Female], June 25, 1963, ADG 162; [Male], May 26, 1963, ADG 112.

This species was common at the Cocoa Research Station. On June 30, 1962, a flock of six was moving through secondary forest. On July 6, 1962, I saw four in dead trees in one of the cocoa fields.

=Mulleripicus pulverulentus pulverulentus= (Temminck): Great Slaty Woodpecker.--Specimen, 1: Tiger Estate: [Male], November 25, 1962, MCT 3326.

I saw this species once at the Cocoa Research Station, where a flock of four was feeding 30 feet up in secondary forest about 100 feet high on October 4, 1962.

=Blythipicus rubiginosus parvus= Chasen and Kloss: Maroon Woodpecker.--Specimens, 2: Cocoa Research Station: [Male], September 28, 1962, MCT 2975. 12 mi. N Kalabakan: [Male] imm., October 17, 1962, MCT 3062.

I saw this bird sporadically while I was on the east coast. It seemed to prefer secondary forest that had some undergrowth and was invariably flushed from the understory.

=Chrysocolaptes validus xanthopygius= Finsch: Orange-backed Woodpecker.--Specimens, 4: Cocoa Research Station: [Male], light body and wing molt, July 2, 1962, MCT 2575; [Male] testis 5 ?3 mm., 168.5 gm., July 23, 1962, MCT 2640; [Female], 176.1 gm., July 23, 1962, MCT 2641; [Male], September 28, 1962, MCT 2976.

This was one of the more common woodpeckers at the Cocoa Research Station. I saw it throughout the period I was there, in secondary forest and dead trees in the cocoa fields.

=Calyptomena viridis gloriosa= Deignan: Green Broadbill.--Specimens, 10: Cocoa Research Station: [Female], 67.4 gm., August 1, 1962, MCT 2698; [Female], 53.2 gm., September 16, 1962, MCT 2927; [Female], May 6, 1963, ADG 106; [Male], June 18, 1963, ADG 148; [Female] by plumage, June 26, 1963, ADG 164. 12 mi. N Kalabakan: [Female], October 12, 1962, MCT 3015; [Female], October 20, 1962, MCT 3098; [Male], October 22, 1962, MCT 3122. Oil Palm Research Station: [Female], August 15, 1963, ADG 240. Pintasan: [Male], October 16, 1963, ADG 310.

Sight records of this species are evidently a poor indication of its abundance, because I saw but one in the field at the Cocoa Research Station, a male sitting in the top of cocoa tree about eight feet up. All the specimens were netted, and the number so taken indicates not only that the species is common but also that it frequents the lower levels of the forest as well as the tops of tall trees (as noted by Smythies, 1960:339).

=Cymbirhynchus macrorhynchus macrorhynchus= (Gmelin): Black-and-Red Broadbill.--Specimens, 2: Kalabakan: [Male], November 16, 1962, MCT 3296. Tiger Estate: [Male], November 25, 1962, MCT 3321.

This species was seen only at Kalabakan, where I caught two in one net in dense secondary forest.

=Eurylaimus ochromalus ochromalus= Raffles: Black-and-Yellow Broadbill.-- Specimens, 9: Cocoa Research Station: [Male], 32.0 gm., July 28, 1962, MCT 2682; [Male], 32.0 gm., August 1, 1962, MCT 2747; [Male], 33.8 gm., August 10, 1962, MCT 2753; [Female], 34.0 gm., September 11, 1962, MCT 2892; [Male], 34.7 gm., September 14, 1962, MCT 2926; [Female], September 26, 1962, MCT 2968; [Male], April 27, 1963, ADG 71. Agricultural Station Gum-Gum: [Female], September 26, 1963, ADG 284. Pintasan Agriculture Station: [Female], October 16, 1963, ADG 311.

This broadbill was common at the Cocoa Research Station in cocoa fields and adjacent secondary forest; it was never seen in primary forest. On September 4, 1962, I saw 10 to 15 in the cocoa, moving in a loose flock. The birds uttered call notes and at the same time bowed their heads sharply, as if to emphasize the call. Frequent supplanting, attacks, and other aggressive interactions were seen. The species was heard and observed also at a place 12 miles north of Kalabakan, at the edge of, but never in, primary forest.

=Eurylaimus javanicus brookei= Robinson and Kloss: Banded Broadbill.-- Specimen, 1: Cocoa Research Station: [Male] testis 7 ?4 mm., 81.8 gm., July

25, 1962, MCT 2660.

This broadbill was seen only on two occasions at the Cocoa Research Station, both times at the edge of the primary forest.

=Pitta baudi= Muller and Schlegel: Blue-headed Pitta.--Specimens, 6: 12 mi. N Kalabakan: [Female], October 17, 1962, MCT 3067; [Female], October 23, 1962, MCT 3131; [Male], October 30, 1962, MCT 3182; [Female], October 30, 1962, MCT 3185; [Female], November 5, 1962, MCT 3212; [Male] testis 4 ?3 mm., November 6, 1962, MCT 3213.

The Blue-headed Pitta was abundant at the Kalabakan collecting locality, in primary forest. It was seen only once at the Cocoa Research Station.

The voice of this bird was a one-note whistle with a terminal inflection. It reminded me of a small child crying. When one called, it was usually in chorus with several others.

=Pitta guajana schwaneri= Bonaparte: Banded Pitta.--Specimens, 4: Cocoa Research Station: [Female] imm, 63.4 gm., July 24, 1962, MCT 2651; [Male] testis 6 ?3 mm., 81.5 gm., August 4, 1962, MCT 2723; [Female] imm., 71.8 gm., August 4, 1962, MCT 2724; [Male], June 15, 1963, ADG 145.

The specimens were taken in primary forest. This pitta was exceedingly tame, often moving along only 20 feet ahead of the observer. The one adult male taken hopped along the forest floor, occasionally jumping up on a log or plant to look back. It finally flushed and flew about 30 feet ahead of me to a log; there it gave a call which can be rendered as shewo, repeated at 10- to 15-second intervals. The call was much like that of Pitta sordida.

=Pitta brachyura moluccensis= (P. L. S. Muller): Blue-winged Pitta.-- Specimen, 1: Tenom: [Female] oviduct slightly enlarged, edematized brood patch, December 31, 1962, MCT 3544.

The specimen was taken in a net stretched across a dry stream near the Padas River in a relatively open area near a coconut grove with some bamboo and elephant ears nearby.

=Pitta sordida mulleri= Bonaparte: Green-breasted Pitta.--Specimens, 2: Cocoa Research Station: [Female], May 1, 1963, ADG 96; [Female], July 15, 1963, ADG 203.

The discovery of this bird by Garcia was a surprise. I was familiar with its habits and calls in the Philippines, and in four months I never heard or observed it at the Cocoa Research Station. Perhaps the specimens were migrants.

=Hirundo tahitica abbotti= Oberholser: Pacific Swallow.--Specimen, 1: Cocoa Research Station: [Male], April 26, 1963, ADG 58.

This species was common at most localities on the east coast. On June 25, 1962, a pair was building a nest under the Cocoa Research Station laboratory. On July 21 young were observed leaving the nest, at the research station rest house.

=Hirundo rustica gutturalis= Scopoli: Common Swallow.--Specimens, 9: 12 mi. N Kalabakan: [Male], November 10, 1962, MCT 3238; [Male], November 10, 1962, MCT 3239; [Female], November 12, 1962, MCT 3257; [Female], November 12, 1962, MCT 3258; [Male], November 12, 1962, MCT 3259; [Female], November 12, 1962, MCT 3260; [Male], November 13, 1962, MCT 3268; [Female], November 13, 1962, MCT 3269; [Female], November 13, 1962, MCT 3270.

I saw this migrant at Semporna on August 19, 1962; soon it was the most common swallow at each of the localities where seen.

=Cecropsia striolata striolata= Temminck and Schlegel: Striated Swallow.-- While in Kalabakan on November 3, 1962, I saw a swallow that differed markedly from others in town. I could not see the breast, but the rump was conspicuously tawny, clearly indicating that the bird belonged to this species. There are but two specimens from Borneo, both from southwestern Sarawak (Smythies, 1960:353). D. M. Batchelor records the species from Kimanis Bay but gives no dates other than November-December (Smythies, 1963:280). Batchelor's observation and mine provide the first records for North Borneo.

=Dicrurus aeneus malayensis= (Blyth): Bronzed Drongo.--Specimen, 1: 12 mi. N Kalabakan: [Female], October 20, 1962, MCT 3104.

This drongo was seen only once, when a flock of three to five was feeding late one evening in a clearing where the trees had been cut down the day before.

=Dicrurus paradiseus brachyphorus= (Bonaparte): Large Racket-tailed Drongo.--Specimens, 5: Cocoa Research Station: [Female] immature, 58.2 gm., August 4, 1962, MCT 2727; [Female], 65.1 gm., August 20, 1962, MCT 2786; [Male], December 1, 1962, MCT 3413. 12 mi. N Kalabakan: [Female], October 20, 1962, MCT 3102. Kalabakan: [Male], November 18, 1962, MCT 3303.

I seldom saw this species in the cocoa at Quoin Hill. Twelve miles north of Kalabakan it was common in tree tops 150 feet up, foraging in the upper canopy.

=Oriolus xanthonotus consobrinus= Ramsay: Malaysian Black-headed Oriole.--Specimens, 9: Cocoa Research Station: [Male] imm., 41.8 gm., July 22, 1962, MCT 2639; [Female], 40.7 gm., July 23, 1962, MCT 2644; [Male] testis 1 ?1 mm., 48.2 gm., July 24, 1962, MCT 2653; [Female] imm., 36.3 gm., July 28, 1962, MCT 2681; [Male] imm., 40.4 gm., August 25, 1962, MCT 2804; [Male], September 26, 1962; MCT 2962; [Male], November 29, 1962, MCT 3381; [Female], December 2, 1962, MCT 3426. 12 mi. N Kalabakan: [Male], October 28, 1962, MCT 3180.

This oriole was common in the cocoa and in secondary forest surrounding the cocoa at Quoin Hill.

=Platylophus galericulatus coronatus= (Raffles): Crested Jay.--Specimens, 4: 12 mi. N Kalabakan: [Female], October 17, 1962, MCT 3068; [Female], October 21, 1962, MCT 3116; [Male], October 21, 1962, MCT 3117; [Male], October 21, 1962, MCT 3118.

This jay was observed several times at the forest camp at Kalabakan. The bird utters a metallic chattering noise much like that of other jays, except for the metallic quality. I observed it also in moss forest 5.5 miles north of Tenom.

Comparison of my specimens with series in the U. S. National Museum and the American Museum of Natural History indicates wide variation within this species in Borneo. The specimens vary considerably in depth of brown, some approaching P. g. lemprieri and others P. g. coronatus. Because of this wide variation I have not recognized the subspecies lemprieri and place all specimens from Borneo under coronatus.

=Platysmurus leucopterus aterrimus= (Temminck): Black Crested Magpie.-- Specimens, 4: Cocoa Research Station: [Female] brood patch refeathering, 181.6 gm., July 21, 1962, MCT 2628; [Female] imm., 143.4 gm., July 21, 1962, MCT 2629; [Female], September 4, 1962, MCT 2865; [Male], 178.0 gm., September 6, 1962, MCT 2880.

The Black Crested Magpie was common at Quoin Hill in secondary forest and cocoa. At the Kalabakan forest camp, I saw a flock of 10 to 20 feeding 70 to 100 feet up in a tree in primary forest.

=Corvus enca compilator= Richmond: Slender-billed Crow.--Specimen, 1: Pintasan Agricultural Station: [Female], October 17, 1963, ADG 315.

Small flocks in the cocoa and secondary forest were common at the Cocoa Research Station.

=Pityriasis gymnocephala= (Temminck): Bald-headed Wood Shrike.--
Specimens, 7: Cocoa Research Station: [Male] one testis, 115.0 gm., October
4, 1962, MCT 2987; [Female] largest ova 15 mm., well-developed brood patch,
oviduct enlarged, 140.0 gm., October 4, 1962, MCT 2988; [Male] testis 8 ?5
mm., 121.0 gm., October 4, 1962, MCT 2989. 12 mi. N Kalabakan: [Male],
November 8, 1962, MCT 3224; [Female], November 8, 1962, MCT 3225;
[Male], November 8, 1962, MCT 3226; [Female], November 8, 1962, MCT
3227.

These birds first drew my attention at Quoin Hill by their peculiar whistle,
which Smythies (1960:491) calls a "nasal whine." They seem not to descend
lower than 30 feet above the ground. They are exceedingly tame; I shot at
them two to four times without frightening them off. They were in badly
disturbed primary forest at Quoin Hill. At a point 12 miles north of Kalabakan,
I found them in primary forest. I took four birds from a flock of five or six.
Later in the afternoon, I heard another group in the tops of trees 150 feet
high. They seemed to be fairly common, judging by the frequency with which
the calls were heard. One of the birds I shot was only wounded and set up
such a clamor that soon the rest of the flock approached, seemingly in
response to the distress calls. Some individuals came within 20 feet of me.
The noise also attracted an accipiter.

Some of the specimens were made into skeletons, which I think show
important indications of the systematic position of this species. The Bald-
headed Wood Shrike has been placed in various families. Gadow (1883:90)
placed it with the Cracticidae, with its closest relative being Cracticus.
Amadon (1956) thought that it was best left in the Prionopidae, with
subfamily status. Hachisuka (1953) concluded that its closest affinities were
with Cracticus of the family Cracticidae. The latest reviser, A. L. Rand (in
Peters et al., 1960:364-365), places it in the Laniidae. A brief comparison of
my skeletons of Pityriasis tended to confirm Gadow's and Hachisuka's
conclusion that it belongs with the Cracticidae. I think that it is best placed in
this family, with subfamily status (Pityriasinae).

=Sitta frontalis corallipes= (Sharpe): Velvet-fronted Nuthatch.--Specimens, 3: Cocoa Research Station: [Female] imm., 14.0 gm., July 23, 1962, MCT 2646; [Male] imm., 13.0 gm., August 20, 1963, MCT 2780; [Male] imm., August 27, 1962, MCT 2820.

I saw several nuthatches feeding in secondary forest at Quoin Hill and one 12 miles north of Kalabakan. One was observed feeding about 100 feet up in a dipterocarp.

=Pellorneum capistratum morrelli= Chasen and Kloss. Black-capped Jungle Babbler.--Specimens, 7: Cocoa Research Station: [Male] testis 3 ?2 mm., 21.1 gm., July 27, 1962, MCT 2667; [Female], 21.4 gm., July 31, 1962, MCT 2690; [Male], September 24, 1962, MCT 2938; [Female], June 13, 1963, ADG 131; [Female] imm., June 14, 1963, ADG 140; [Female], July 7, 1963, ADG 168. Ulu Balung Cocoa Estate: [Female], July 11, 1963, ADG 188.

This species was seen 12 miles north of Kalabakan and at Quoin Hill. It was fairly common and could be seen running on the ground ahead of the observer, occasionally hopping up on a brush pile or branch, seemingly to make a quick survey before moving back to the ground. It preferred primary forest but was occasionally observed in the primary-secondary forest edge vegetation.

=Trichastoma pyrrhogenys canicapillum= (Sharpe): Temminck Jungle Babbler.--Specimens, 13: 5.5 mi. SW Tenom: [Female], December 17, 1962, MCT 3445; [Male], December 17, 1962, MCT 3446; [Male], December 17, 1962, MCT 3452; [Male], December 18, 1962, MCT 34554; [Female] collapsed follicles, brood patch, December 18, 1962, MCT 3455; [Male], December 18, 1962, MCT 3460; [Male] testis 2 ?1 mm., December 18, 1962, MCT 3461; [Male], December 19, 1962, MCT 3474; [Male] testis 6 ?3 mm., December 19, 1962, MCT 3475; [Male], December 22, 1962, MCT 3505; [Male], December 24, 1962, MCT 3528; [Female] imm., December 25, 1962, MCT 3532; [Male] testis 5 ?3 mm., December 25, 1962, MCT 3533.

This species was common in the moss forest near Tenom. The female specimen with collapsed follicles indicates that some of the birds were in breeding condition. All specimens were netted.

=Trichastoma malaccense poliogenys= (Strickland): Short-tailed Jungle Babbler.--Specimens, 17: Cocoa Research Station: [Male] testis 7 ?4 mm., 24.5 gm., July 31, 1962, MCT 2687; [Female], September 5, 1962, MCT 2874; [Female], September 24, 1962, MCT 2941; [Male], November 29, 1962, MCT 3387; [Female], November 29, 1962, MCT 3388; [Male], December 1, 1962, MCT 3400; [Female], November 12, 1962, MCT 3262. Kalabakan: [Male], November 16, 1962, MCT 3292. Cocoa Research Station: [Male], June 11, 1963, ADG 123; [Male], June 12, 1963, ADG 127; [Female], June 13, 1963, ADG 132. Ulu Balung Cocoa Estate: [Male], July 9, 1963, ADG 179; [Male], July 9, 1963, ADG 179 (sic). Oil Palm Research Station: [Male], August 10, 1963, ADG 219; [Male], August 12, 1963, ADG 225; [Female], August 13, 1963, ADG 236; [Female], August 23, 1963, ADG 255.

This terrestrial species was common in primary forest, and occasionally in secondary forest, in low trees or around brush piles. On September 24, by "squeaking," I so aroused one bird that it ran back and forth on a limb of a fallen tree in great agitation. The specimen taken on November 12 was in heavy molt; it lacked tail feathers and the primaries were being replaced.

=Trichastoma bicolor= (Lesson): Ferruginous Jungle Babbler.--Specimens, 6: 12 mi. N Kalabakan: [Male], October 24, 1962, MCT 3143; [Female], October 26, 1962, MCT 3161; [Male], November 10, 1962, MCT 3135; [Female], November 12, 1962, MCT 3255. Oil Palm Research Station: [Male], August 12, 1963, ADG 266; [Female], August 28, 1963, ADG 269.

All specimens were taken in primary forest.

=Trichastoma sepiarium harteri= (Chasen and Kloss): Horsfield Jungle Babbler.--Specimens, 6: Cocoa Research Station: [Male] testis 8 ?5 mm., 25.7 gm., July 24, 1962, MCT 2652; [Male] testis 8 ?5 mm., 28.2 gm., July 27, 1962,

MCT 2668; [Male] testis 8 ?7 mm., 28.2 gm., July 31, 1962, MCT 2688; [Male], June 15, 1963, ADG 142. 12 mi. N Kalabakan: [Male] testis 8 ?5 mm., November 8, 1962, MCT 3233. Oil Palm Research Station: [Female], September 5, 1963, ADG 275.

This babbler tends to inhabit secondary growth more than does T. malaccense and was partly arboreal, occasionally ranging as high as 20 feet above ground. It occurred occasionally in flocks of four or five.

=Malacopteron magnum magnum= Eyton: Greater Red-headed Babbler.-- Specimens, 12: Cocoa Research Station: [Male] testis 7 ?5 mm., September 7, 1962, MCT 2886; [Male] testis 9 ?5 mm., October 4, 1962, MCT 2990; [Male], November 30, 1962, MCT 3437; [Female], November 27, 1962, MCT 3340; [Female], April 30, 1963, ADG 91; [Male], June 14, 1963, ADG 136; [Male], July 9, 1963, ADG 178. Ulu Balung Cocoa Estate: [Male], July 11, 1963, ADG 191; [Male], July 16, 1963, ADG 205. 12 mi. N Kalabakan: [Male], October 22, 1962, MCT 3124; [Female], October 28, 1962, MCT 3176; [Male], October 28, 1962, MCT 3177.

This babbler was common at the Cocoa Research Station but uncommon elsewhere. It seemed to prefer primary forest and was only rarely seen in the cocoa. My series shows that this species was common at Quoin Hill and M. cinereum was rare, while the opposite obtained 12 miles north of Kalabakan. For the moment this cannot be explained. Possibly these two species are competitive and tend toward mutual exclusion. Since the birds were mostly netted, it is assumed that I obtained a random sample. My observations at Quoin Hill seem to bear out the specimen record.

The specimens in my series of M. m. magnum are more nearly black on the crown than those labelled M. m. saba in the U. S. National Museum (from the Segah River), but there was much variation in the amount of black on the crown in all series examined. I consider M. m. saba to be synonymous with M. m. magnum.

=Malacopteron cinereum cinereum= Eyton: Lesser Red-headed Babbler.--Specimens, 29: Cocoa Research Station: [Male], December 2, 1962, MCT 3428; [Female], June 11, 1963, ADG 124; [Male], July 9, 1963, ADG 178. 12 mi. N Kalabakan: [Male], October 13, 1962, MCT 3025; [Female], October 13, 1962, MCT 3030; [Male], October 13, 1962, MCT 3032; [Female], October 14, 1962, MCT 3042; [Male], October 14, 1962, MCT 3043; [Female], October 16, 1962, MCT 3059; [Male], October 21, 1962, MCT 3119; [Male], October 22, 1962, MCT 3128; [Female], October 24, 1962, MCT 3136; [Male], October 28, 1962, MCT 3178; sex?, October 31, 1962, MCT 3188; [Female], November 7, 1962, MCT 3219; [Female], November 7, 1962, MCT 3220; [Male], November 12, 1962, MCT 3263; [Female], November 12, 1962, MCT 3264. Kalabakan: [Male], November 15, 1962, MCT 3282; [Male], November 15, 1962, MCT 3284; [Female], November 15, 1962, MCT 3285. Ulu Balung Cocoa Estate: [Male], July 13, 1963, ADG 197. Oil Palm Research Station: sex?, August 16, 1963, ADG 245; [Female], August 28, 1963, ADG 272. Pintasan Agriculture Station: [Male], October 17, 1963, ADG 318; [Male], October 18, 1963, ADG 319; [Male], October 18, 1963, ADG 320; [Female], October 18, 1963, ADG 321; [Female], October 18, 1963, ADG 322. See remarks under M. magnum.

=Malacopteron magnirostre cinereocapillum= (Salvadori): Brown-headed Babbler.--Specimens, 20: Cocoa Research Station: [Male] testis 5 ?3 mm., 20.4 gm., July 23, 1962, MCT 2647; [Male] testis 2 ?1 mm., 20.0 gm., July 24, 1962, MCT 2656; [Male] testis 1 ?1 mm., 20.5 gm., July 24, 1962, MCT 2657; [Male], 20.4 gm., July 27, 1962, MCT 2669. 12 mi. N Kalabakan: [Male], October 10, 1962, MCT 2994; [Male] testis 5 ?3 mm., October 12, 1962, MCT 3016; [Female], October 12, 1962, MCT 3017; [Male], October 13, 1962, MCT 3026; [Female], October 13, 1962, MCT 3028; [Male], October 17, 1962, MCT 3070; [Male], October 19, 1962, MCT 3083; [Male], October 19, 1962, MCT 3084; [Male] testis 5 ?4 mm., October 20, 1962, MCT 3108; [Male], October 26, 1962, MCT 3158; [Female], October 26, 1962, MCT 3159; [Male], November 11, 1962, MCT 3253; [Female], November 11, 1962, MCT 3254. 5.5 mi. SW Tenom: [Male], December 19, 1962, MCT 3462. Oil Palm Research Station: [Female], August 28, 1963, ADG 265.

This babbler inhabits the understory of primary forest, and occasionally is seen in secondary forest scrub. A specimen was taken at 4,000 feet elevation in moss forest near Tenom. The breeding season is seemingly in June and July but there is indication of gonadal activity in males in October (MCT 3108). On October 15, 1962, I observed an individual feeding on the rough bark of a large dipterocarp. The bird was clinging to the bark much as a nuthatch would, hopping along the vertical trunk upside down, laterally and straight up. Other birds of the species were feeding close by in small trees about 20 feet tall.

=Pomatorhinus montanus borneensis= Cabanis: Chestnut-backed Scimitar Babbler.--Specimens, 3: Cocoa Research Station: [Male] testis 5 ?2 mm., 33.1 gm., July 23, 1962, MCT 2643; [Male] testis 2 ?1 mm., 28.2 gm., July 24, 1962, MCT 2655. 5.5 mi. SW Tenom: [Male], December 22, 1962, MCT 3496.

This bird of the understory in primary forest was seen in only one other situation, 12 miles north of Kalabakan it was feeding in a clearing near our camp.

=Ptilocichla leucogrammica= (Bonaparte): Bornean Wren-babbler.-- Specimens, 3: Ulu Balung Cocoa Estate: [Male], July 17, 1963, ADG 207: [Female] one egg in oviduct, July 19, 1963, ADG 211. Oil Palm Research Station: [Female] egg in oviduct, August 13, 1963, ADG 230.

Garcia netted three specimens in primary forest. This bird is known from Borneo only from a few specimens (Smythies, 1960:410). In North Borneo, it has been known previously only from Bettotan on the east coast (Smythies, 1960:410). The additional records published herewith also are for the east coast.

=Kenopia striata= (Blyth): Striped Wren-babbler.--Specimens, 11: Cocoa Research Station: [Female], 21.1 gm., July 24, 1962, MCT 2649; [Male] testis 4 ?3 mm., 19.6 gm., July 24, 1962, MCT 2640; [Male] testis 2 ?1 mm., 18.7 gm., July 27, 1962, MCT 2670. 12 mi. N Kalabakan: [Female], October 28, 1962, MCT 3172; [Male], October 21, 1962, MCT 3114; [Female], October 22, 1962,

MCT 3123; [Male], October 26, 1962, MCT 3157; [Male], October 30, 1962, MCT 3187; [Male], November 1, 1962, MCT 3192. Ulu Balung Cocoa Estate: [Male], July 21, 1963, ADG 213. Oil Palm Research Station: [Male], August 13, 1963, ADG 229; [Female], August 19, 1963, ADG 250.

This bird of primary forest is found occasionally in adjacent secondary forest and spends about three-fourths of its time running about on the ground, only occasionally ascending to the lower branches of trees. The song may be rendered as kittle jank, the first note being trilled and a bit higher than the last, which is short and chopped off. This babbler appears to sing as it moves along the forest floor without stopping. It was observed foraging under leaves, and was common both at Quoin Hill and 12 miles north of Kalabakan, in groups of two or three birds.

=Macronous gularis= (Horsfield): Striped Tit-babbler.--I saw this bird at the Semporna Rest House feeding in shrubbery. It was not seen elsewhere.

=Macronous ptilosus reclusus= Hartert: Fluffy-backed Tit-babbler.-- Specimens, 2: Kalabakan: [Male], November 15, 1962, MCT 3283. Oil Palm Research Station: sex?, August 23, 1963, ADG 254.

This bird was seen only at Kalabakan, in dense secondary growth. My specimen was in heavy molt.

=Stachyris nigriceps hartleyi= Chasen: Gray-throated Tree Babbler.-- Specimens, 16: 5.5 mi. SW Tenom: [Male], December 17, 1962, MCT 3451; [Female], December 18, 1962, MCT 3456; [Male] testis 7 ?5 mm., December 18, 1962, MCT 3457; [Male] testis 6 ?3 mm., December 18, 1962, MCT 3458; [Female], December 18, 1962, MCT 3459; [Female] old brood patch, December 19, 1962, MCT 3471; [Male] testis 9 ?5 mm., December 19, 1962, MCT 3472; [Female] several collapsed follicles, December 19, 1962, MCT 3473; [Male] testis 6 ?4 mm., December 20, 1962, MCT 3480; [Male] testis enlarged, December 20, 1962, MCT 3481; [Female] imm., December 20, 1962, MCT 3482; [Male] testis 7 ?5 mm., December 20, 1962, MCT 3486; [Female],

December 21, 1962, MCT 3493; [Male] testis 7 ?5 mm., December 21, 1962, MCT 3494; [Female] imm., December 21, 1962, MCT 3495; [Female] imm., December 22, 1962, MCT 3506.

This babbler was abundant in the moss forest above Tenom and appeared to be at the height of its breeding season in December.

The specimens were compared with material at the American Museum of Natural History and proved to be S. n. hartleyi, which has not previously been reported from North Borneo.

=Stachyris poliocephala= (Temminck): Gray-headed Tree Babbler.-- Specimens, 8: Cocoa Research Station: [Male] testis 3 ?2 mm., 24.0 gm., July 28, 1962, MCT 2674; [Male], December 1, 1962, MCT 3414; [Female], December 1, 1962, MCT 3415. 12 mi. N Kalabakan: [Female], October 18, 1962, MCT 3072; sex?, October 29, 1962, MCT 3181; [Female], November 2, 1962, MCT 3202. Oil Palm Research Station: [Male], August 16, 1963, ADG 248; [Female], August 15, 1962, ADG 239.

This species of the secondary forest usually was associated with piles of brush or heavy growth of fern. I never saw it higher than three feet above the ground.

=Stachyris nigricollis= (Temminck): Black-necked Tree Babbler.--Specimens, 4: Cocoa Research Station: [Male], June 15, 1963, ADG 144. Ulu Balung Cocoa Estate: [Female], July 15, 1963, ADG 201. Oil Palm Research Station: [Male], August 12, 1963, ADG 224; [Female], August 19, 1963, ADG 251.

Although I worked in the same area and at the same time of year as did Garcia, I did not see this species.

=Stachyris leucotis obscurata= Mayr: White-necked Tree Babbler.--Specimen, 1: Oil Palm Research Station: [Male], September 5, 1963, ADG 274.

Garcia's specimen was taken in primary forest. Smythies (1960:418) states that most records come from submontane localities, except for those from Bettotan; the specimen is from an altitude of 40 feet, near Bettotan.

=Stachyris maculata maculata= (Temminck): Red-rumped Tree Babbler.-- Specimens, 12: Cocoa Research Station: [Female] largest ova 2 mm., brood patch, July 10, 1962, MCT 2613; [Male], 25.8 gm., August 5, 1962, MCT 2731; [Male], 28.0 gm., August 5, 1962, MCT 2732. 12 mi. N Kalabakan: [Male] testis 3 ?3 mm., October 12, 1962, MCT 3006; [Female], October 12, 1962, MCT 3007; [Female], October 12, 1962, MCT 3008; [Male], October 12, 1962, MCT 3009. Cocoa Research Station: [Female], June 11, 1963, ADG 121; [Female], June 13, 1963, ADG 133; [Male], June 14, 1963, ADG 134. Oil Palm Research Station: [Female], August 14, 1963, ADG 235; [Female], August 15, 1963, ADG 237.

This babbler was common in small groups at Quoin Hill. Whitehead (1893:227) states that the species "frequents the true forest near the ground." I observed these babblers only in sub-canopy trees, at least 30 feet above the ground. Smythies (1960:419) stated that he had never seen this species in the forest undergrowth.

=Stachyris erythroptera bicolor= (Blyth): Red-winged Tree Babbler.-- Specimens, 11: Cocoa Research Station: [Male] testis 2 ?1 mm., 13.4 gm., July 24, 1962, MCT 2654; [Female] imm., 13.0 gm., August 28, 1962, MCT 2832; [Female], 12.5 gm., August 28, 1962, MCT 2833; [Male], December 2, 1962, MCT 3432; [Female], December 2, 1962, MCT 3433. 12 mi. N Kalabakan: [Male], October 10, 1962, MCT 2995; [Male], November 6, 1962, MCT 3215; [Male], November 7, 1962, MCT 3218. 5.5 mi. SW Tenom: [Male] testis 3 ?1 mm., December 18, 1962, MCT 3463. Ulu Balung Cocoa Estate: [Male], July 10, 1963, ADG 184; [Male], July 17, 1963, ADG 206.

This species was seen most often in primary forest undergrowth, but occasionally as high as 10 feet up in small trees. I saw it also in and around brush piles in secondary forest. The one specimen from 5.5 mi. SW Tenom was taken in the moss forest. MCT 2833 was in heavy molt on the wings, head, and body.

=Stachyris rufifrons sarawacensis= Chasen: Hume's Tree Babbler.--Specimen, 1: Cocoa Research Station: [Male] testis 4 ?3 mm., November 28, 1962, MCT 3358.

There was no comparative material in the U. S. National Museum where I studied the specimen but it fits Chasen's original description of S. r. sarawacensis. H. G. Deignan (in Peters et al., 1964:303) considered this subspecies doubtfully distinct from S. r. poliogaster.

The specimen was taken at a height of one and one-half feet in a mist net set along a path. The bird was caught when it attempted to cross the path from a patch of heavy undergrowth to a patch on the other side. Mary Norman observed them at Kalabakan (Smythies, 1963:281) in saplings. They should probably be considered birds of the understory.

=Alcippe brunneicauda= (Salvadori): Brown Quaker Babbler.--Specimens, 22: Cocoa Research Station: [Male] imm., 14.4 gm., August 20, 1962, MCT 2781; [Female], 14.9 gm., September 6, 1962, MCT 2877; [Female], September 25, 1962, MCT 2957; [Female], November 28, 1962, MCT 3361; [Female], November 28, 1962, MCT 3362; [Male], November 28, 1962, MCT 3376; [Male], November 28, 1962, MCT 3378; [Male] testis 5 ?3 mm., December 1, 1962, MCT 3410; [Male], December 2, 1962, MCT 3435; [Male], November 30, 1962, MCT 3440; [Male], November 30, 1962, MCT 3441. 12 mi. N Kalabakan: sex?, November 1, 1962, MCT 3194; [Male], November 11, 1962, MCT 3243; [Male], November 11, 1962, MCT 3245; [Male], November 11, 1962, MCT 3247; [Male], November 11, 1962, MCT 3248; [Male], November 12, 1962, MCT 3261; [Female], November 13, 1962, MCT 3267; [Female], November 10, 1962, MCT 3306. 5.5 mi. SW Tenom: [Female], December 22, 1962, MCT 3501; [Female], December 22, 1962, MCT 3502; [Female], December 22, 1962, MCT 3503.

Birds of this species were common in primary forest at the three localities listed under "specimens." They travel in small, loose flocks, calling as they move through the forest. Periodic calling, interspersed with periods of silence, was characteristic of the species; vocalization of this sort may function in maintaining the unity of the well spaced flock.

=Yuhina castaniceps everetti= (Sharpe): Chestnut-headed Yuhina.--Specimens, 14: 5.5 mi. SW Tenom: [Female], December 19, 1962, MCT 3468; [Male] testis 6 ?3 mm., December 23, 1962, MCT 3512; [Male] testis 7 ?3 mm., December 23, 1962, MCT 3513; [Male] testis 6 ?3 mm., December 24, 1962, MCT 3520; [Female], December 24, 1962, MCT 3521; [Male] testis 5 ?3 mm., December 24, 1962, MCT 3523; [Male] testis 6 ?3 mm., December 24, 1962, MCT 3524; [Female], December 24, 1962, MCT 3525; [Female], December 24, 1962, MCT 3526; [Male] testis 6 ?3 mm., December 24, 1962, MCT 3527; [Male] testis 6 ?3 mm., December 28, 1962, MCT 3542; [Male] testis 6 ?3 mm., December 28, 1962, MCT 3543.

I saw several flocks of this species in moss forest at a point 5.5 miles southwest of Tenom. Some were observed going into cavities in the moss, where they apparently caught insects. They sometimes did this simultaneously, in several places on the same tree.

=Yuhina zantholeuca brunnescens= (Sharpe): White-bellied Yuhina.--Specimens, 4: 12 mi. N Kalabakan: [Female], October 12, 1962, MCT 3010; sex?, November 1, 1962, MCT 3193; sex?, December 22, 1962, MCT 3500; [Male] testis 7 ?4 mm., December 23, 1962, MCT 3519.

One flock of about five of these yuhinas was seen in primary forest at Kalabakan. Another small group was observed in the moss forest near Tenom.

=Tephrodornis gularis frenatus= Betikofer: Hook-billed Graybird.--Specimens, 3: Cocoa Research Station: [Male], September 25, 1962, wing molt, MCT 2946; [Female], September 25, 1962, wing molt, MCT 2947; [Female], September 25, 1962, MCT 2948.

I observed this species twice in six months on the east coast. The three collected at the research station in the cocoa were in a family group. On November 9, 1962, I saw three birds feeding at the edge of the primary forest.

=Coracina striata sumatrensis= (S. Muller): Barred Graybird.--Specimens, 2: Tiger Estate: [Female], December 30, 1962; [Male], December 30, 1962.

=Coracina fimbriata schierbrandi= (Pelzeln): Lesser Graybird.--Specimens, 6: Cocoa Research Station: [Male] imm., 25.7 gm., July 22, 1962, MCT 2637; sex?, 29.5 gm., July 28, 1962, MCT 2676; [Male], 28.4 gm., August 5, 1962, MCT 2729; [Female], 30.0 gm., September 13, 1962, MCT 2917. 12 mi. N Kalabakan: [Female], October 25, 1962, MCT 3147. Tiger Estate: [Male], November 25, 1962, MCT 3317.

This species was common at the Cocoa Research Station, most common in the cocoa, and an occasional bird was observed in the primary forest.

The adult male (MCT 3317) from Tiger Estate was darker than any in the series of C. f. schierbrandi in The American Museum of Natural History, and closely approached a series C. f. culminata from Malaya in the same museum.

=Hemipus hirundinaceus= (Temminck): Black-winged Flycatcher Shrike.-- Specimen, 1: Cocoa Research Station: [Female], 10.2 gm., July 21, 1962, MCT 2632.

The specimen was taken in the cocoa where it was sitting on a dead limb, occasionally darting out after insects, and provides the only record from this locality. At the collecting site 12 miles north of Kalabakan, however, it was seen several times feeding in small flocks in a clearing near a trail.

=Hemipus picatus intermedius= Salvadori: Bar-winged Flycatcher Shrike.-- Specimens, 6: Cocoa Research Station: [Female] imm., August 27, 1962, MCT 2815; [Male] imm., August 27, 1962, MCT 2816; [Female], August 27, 1962,

MCT 2817; [Female], 9.8 gm., September 12, 1962, MCT 2906; [Female], 10.2 gm., September 12, 1962, MCT 2907; [Male] imm., 8.7 gm., September 12, 1962, MCT 2908.

Smythies (1960:362) lists this species as a montane resident. However, the elevation of the Cocoa Research Station is only 750 feet, which is clearly submontane (Smythies, 1960:693). I saw the birds in a flock of three or four, feeding in shade trees in the cocoa fields. They acted like typical flycatchers, sitting on twigs and darting out after insects. On September 12, a flock of 10 was seen in the same area. Whitehead (1893:208) described the habits of the species as being like those of Tephrodornis gularis and not at all like those of a flycatcher.

=Lalage nigra= (Forster): Pied Triller.--Common in the lowlands near Tawau and Tuaran. On September 19, 1962, I saw an adult feeding one young on Siamil Island.

=Pericrocotus igneus igneus= Blyth: Fiery Minivet.--Specimens, 3: Cocoa Research Station: [Male], 15.8 gm., August 11, 1962, MCT 2764; [Male], 14.0 gm., August 11, 1962, MCT 2766; [Female], 15.2 gm., August 11, 1962, MCT 2767.

I saw this species only on August 11, 1962, when a flock of eight was seen feeding in a cocoa tree.

The female is somewhat darker than comparative material from Borneo, possibly owing to fresh plumage in my specimen and foxing in the older comparative material.

=Pericrocotus flammeus insulanus= Deignan: Scarlet Minivet.--Specimens, 5: Cocoa Research Station: [Male] testis 2 ?1 mm., 20.0 gm., July 7, 1962, MCT 2608; [Female], 19.7 gm., August 4, 1962, MCT 2728; [Male], 19.0 gm., August 23, 1962, MCT 2802. Tiger Estate: [Female], June 23, 1963, ADG 160; [Male], June 23, 1963, ADG 161.

This minivet was common at the Cocoa Research Station, where it usually inhabited the shade trees in the cocoa groves. The birds seen and the one taken on July 7 were all in heavy molt.

=Pycnonotus eutilotus= (Jardine and Selby): Crested Brown Bulbul.-- Specimens, 2: Cocoa Research Station: [Female], December 2, 1962, MCT 3421; [Male], June 19, 1963, ADG 152.

The species was netted twice in much disturbed primary forest.

=Pycnonotus melanoleucos= (Eyton): Black and White Bulbul.--Specimen, 1: 12 mi. N Kalabakan: [Female], November 5, 1962, MCT 3211.

The specimen was caught in a mist net in primary forest. It was aberrant; the two outer tail feathers were white and it had a few white under tail coverts.

=Pycnonotus squamatus borneensis= Chasen: Scaly-breasted Bulbul.-- Specimens, 2: Cocoa Research Station: [Female] 24.0 gm., August 2, 1962, MCT 2708; [Male] testis 4 ?3 mm., 22.2 gm., August 23, 1962, MCT 2802.

Both specimens were taken from a feeding tree, Trema orientalis, in which they were eating berries. This species of tree was used for shade in the cocoa.

=Pycnonotus cyaniventris paroticalis= (Sharpe): Gray-bellied Bulbul.-- Specimens, 2: Cocoa Research Station: [Female] largest ovum 2 mm., 21.6 gm., August 25, 1962, MCT 2808; [Male] testis 7 ?4 mm., 20.5 gm., September 13, 1962, MCT 2916.

On August 23, 1962, I saw four in the cocoa but they took flight into the forest. I later collected two specimens from a shade tree, Trema orientalis, in which they were feeding upon the berries.

=Pycnonotus atriceps atriceps= (Temminck): Black-headed Bulbul.--
Specimens, 9: Cocoa Research Station: [Female], April 29, 1963, ADG 85;
[Female], April 27, 1963, ADG 72; [Female], April 20, 1963, ADG 90; [Male],
April 27, 1963, ADG 69; [Male], April 28, 1963, ADG 79; [Male], April 26, 1963,
ADG 61; [Male], April 28, 1963, ADG 81; [Male] juv., April 28, 1963, ADG 82;
[Male], May 1, 1963, ADG 97.

I did not see this species in my stay at the Cocoa Research Station, and the
specimens taken by Garcia constitute the only record. The juvenal plumage in
one specimen indicates that the species breeds at Quoin Hill.

=Pycnonotus zeylanicus= (Gmelin): Yellow-crowned Bulbul.--It was common
at Tuaran.

=Pycnonotus goiavier gourdini= Gray 1847: Yellow-vented Bulbul.--
Specimens, 17: Tenom: [Female], December 31, 1962, MCT 3547; [Male]
testis 9 ?6 mm., December 31, 1962, MCT 3548; [Female] oviduct regressing,
old brood patch, December 31, 1962, MCT 3549; [Male], December 31, 1962,
MCT 3550; [Female] oviduct nearly regressed, January 1, 1963, MCT 3556;
[Female], January 1, 1963, MCT 3557; [Male] testis 9 ?7 mm., December 31,
1963, MCT 3558; [Male] testis enlarged, January 1, 1963, MCT 3559; [Female],
January 1, 1963, MCT 3560; [Male], January 2, 1963, MCT 3562; [Female],
January 2, 1963, MCT 3566; [Male], January 2, 1963, MCT 3567; [Male] testis
9 ?7 mm., January 2, 1963, MCT 3568; [Male], January 2, 1963, MCT 3569;
[Female], January 2, 1963, MCT 3570; [Female], January 2, 1963, MCT 3571;
[Male] testis 9 ?7 mm., January 2, 1963, MCT 3572.

Although this species was observed by me at the Cocoa Research Station, I
was unable to obtain any specimens. It was also seen commonly at Semporna,
Siamil Island, Kalabakan, Brantian Estate, and at Tuaran, always associated
with cultivated areas. The birds obviously were breeding at Tenom in
December, and several young were taken. In some, the molt of the wings,
body, and tail had begun.

=Pycnonotus plumosus hutzi= Stresemann: Large Olive Bulbul.--Specimens, 8: Tenom: [Female], December 31, 1962, MCT 3551; [Male] testis 6 ?5 mm., January 1, 1963, MCT 3553; [Male] testis small, January 1, 1963, MCT 3554; [Male] testis 6 ?4 mm., January 4, 1963, MCT 3577; [Male] testis 5 ?4 mm., January 4, 1963, MCT 3578. Mt. Rumas: [Male], March 6, 1963, ADG 16; [Female], March 6, 1963, ADG 17; sex?, March 6, 1963, ADG 15.

The specimens were netted in scrub-grassland at Tenom. The size of the testes of the Tenom specimens indicated that the birds were breeding.

=Pycnonotus brunneus brunneus= Blyth: Red-eyed Brown Bulbul.-- Specimens, 17: Cocoa Research Station: [Male] imm., 32.6 gm., July 22, 1962, MCT 2638; [Male] testis minute, 37.3 gm., August 2, 1962, MCT 2709; [Male] testis minute, 36.0 gm., August 3, 1962, MCT 2720; [Female] ovary granular, September 4, 1962, MCT 2867; [Male] testis 6 ?4 mm., September 4, 1962, MCT 2868; [Female] egg in oviduct, largest ovum 9 mm., 1 collapsed follicle, 30.0 gm., September 10, 1962, MCT 2894; [Male] testis small, September 25, 1962, MCT 2953; [Female], September 25, 1962, MCT 2954; [Male] testis small, November 27, 1962, MCT 3346; [Male] testis 4 ?2 mm., November 29, 1962, MCT 3380; [Male] testis small, November 29, 1962 MCT 3393; [Male] testis small, December 1, 1962, MCT 3402; [Male] testis small, December 1, 1962, MCT 3403; [Male] testis small, December 1, 1962, MCT 3404; [Female] ovary minute, December 1, 1962, MCT 3416; [Male] testis small, November 30, 1962, MCT 3438. Oil Palm Research Station: [Female], August 27, 1963, ADG 260.

This most common of the "brown" bulbuls at the Cocoa Research Station frequented shade trees (Trema orientalis). One bird fed on small red peppers, Capsicum sp. Some of the September-taken specimens were in breeding condition.

=Pycnonotus simplex perplexus= Chasen and Kloss: White-eyed Brown Bulbul.--Specimens, 3: 5.5 mi. SW Tenom: [Female] ovary granular, December 19, 1962, MCT 3469; [Male] testis 4 ?3 mm., December 20, 1962, MCT 3478;

[Female] ovary granular, December 22, 1962, MCT 3499.

This bird was taken only in the moss forest at 4,000 feet elevation near Tenom. Smythies (1960:382) considered the species to be characteristic of the lowlands. Specimens were taken by Harrison in the Kelabit Uplands (Smythies, 1957:704) at 4,200 feet.

=Pycnonotus erythrophthalmos salvadori= (Sharpe): Lesser Olive-brown Bulbul.--Specimens, 15: Cocoa Research Station: [Male] testis 6 ?4 mm., 20.2 gm., August 12, 1962, MCT 2778; [Male] testis 6 ?5 mm., 19.8 gm., August 28, 1962, MCT 2830; [Female] ovary granular, 20.5 gm., August 28, 1962, MCT 2831; [Female] imm., 20.0 gm., September 14, 1962, MCT 2925; [Male] testis 7 ?5 mm., September 25, 1962, MCT 2928; [Male]?, October 2, 1962, MCT 2983; [Female], November 27, 1962, MCT 3357; [Male] testis small, December 1, 1962, MCT 3405; [Male] testis minute, December 2, 1962, MCT 3420; [Male] testis small, December 1, 1962, MCT 3434; [Male] testis small, November 30, 1962, MCT 3439; [Female], April 26, 1962, ADG 63; [Male], July 7, 1963, ADG 170; [Male], July 7, 1963, ADG 171; [Male], July 8, 1963, ADG 176.

This species commonly fed in the shade trees (Trema orientalis), along with other species of bulbuls. I occasionally saw individuals in primary forest.

=Criniger bres gutturalis= (Bonaparte): Olive White-throated Bulbul.-- Specimens, 25: Cocoa Research Station: [Female] ovary regressed, 41.4 gm., July 27, 1962, MCT 2666; [Female], 46.0 gm., July 28, 1962, MCT 2672; [Male], 51.2 gm., July 31, 1962, heavy molt, MCT 2685; [Male] testis 4 ?3 mm., 52.6 gm., August 2, 1962, MCT 2710; [Male], November 27, 1962, MCT 3353; [Female], November 27, 1962, MCT 3354; [Female], June 14, 1963, ADG 138; [Female], July 8, 1963, ADG 172; [Male], July 7, 1963, ADG 173; sex?, July 11, 1963, ADG 190. 12 mi. N Kalabakan: [Female], October 16, 1962, MCT 3052; [Male] testis small, October 22, 1962, MCT 3127; [Male], October 24, 1962, MCT 3137; sex?, November 1, 1962, MCT 3190; [Female], November 2, 1962, MCT 3201; [Female], November 11, 1962, MCT 3250; [Male] testis small,

November 13, 1962, MCT 3271; [Female], November 17, 1962, MCT 3301. Oil Palm Research Station: [Female], August 16, 1963, ADG 246; [Female] juvenal, August 19, 1963, ADG 253; [Female], August 23, 1963, ADG 256; [Female], August 28, 1963, ADG 264; [Male], August 28, 1963, ADG 270; [Female], August 28, 1963, ADG 271; [Female], October 4, 1963, ADG 293.

At the Cocoa Research Station this species was common and inhabited the cocoa and surrounding secondary forest. I found it to be common 12 miles north of Kalabakan.

=Criniger ochraceous ruficrissus= Sharpe: Brown White-throated Bulbul.-- Specimens, 5: 5.5 mi. SW Tenom: [Female], December 21, 1962, MCT 3489; [Male] testis 3 ?2 mm., December 21, 1962, MCT 3490; [Male] testis 4 ?3 mm., December 21, 1962, MCT 3491; [Female], December 23, 1962, MCT 3518; [Female], December 25, 1962, MCT 3535.

This bird was seen only in the moss forest above Tenom. It was not taken in nets the first four days they were erected, nor did we see individuals in the forest. Then, on December 21, three were taken in widely separated nets, and the species was then seen nearly every day for a week. Such sporadic and unpredictable local occurrences may indicate wide separation of the loosely-organized foraging groups of this species. The call is a harsh, jaylike note.

=Criniger phaeocephalus connectens= (Chasen and Kloss): Crestless White-throated Bulbul.--Specimens, 31: Cocoa Research Station: [Female], December 1, 1962, MCT 3406; [Male] testis 5 ?4 mm., 35.0 gm., July 31, 1962, MCT 2689; [Male], May 2, 1963, ADG 104; [Male], June 22, 1963, ADG 122. 12 mi. N Kalabakan: [Male] testis 6 ?4 mm., October 12, 1962, MCT 3002; [Female], October 12, 1962, MCT 3003; [Female], October 12, 1962, MCT 3004; [Male], October 14, 1962, MCT 3037; [Male], October 14, 1962, MCT 3038; [Female], October 14, 1962, MCT 3039; [Female], October 17, 1962, MCT 3063; [Male], October 17, 1962, MCT 3071; [Male], October 19, 1962, MCT 3080; [Male], October 20, 1962, MCT 3106; [Male], October 20, 1962, MCT 3110; [Male], October 21, 1962, MCT 3115; [Female], October 22, 1962,

MCT 3125; [Female] October 23, 1962, MCT 3135; [Female], October 24, 1962, MCT 3142; [Female], October 26, 1962, MCT 3155; [Male], October 28, 1962, MCT 3175; sex?, October 30, 1962, MCT 3186; [Female], November 1, 1962, MCT 3191; [Male], November 8, 1962, heavy molt, MCT 3234. Kalabakan: [Female], November 15, 1962, heavy molt, MCT 3288. 5.5 mi. SW Tenom: [Female], December 17, 1962, MCT 3453. Oil Palm Research Station: [Male], August 15, 1963, ADG 241; [Male], August 27, 1963, ADG 259; [Male], September 5, 1963, ADG 276. Gum-Gum: [Male], September 4, 1963, ADG 283. Lamag: [Male], October 15, 1963, ADG 308.

This species of the primary forest was common both at Cocoa Research Station and 12 miles north of Kalabakan. Although not frequently seen, it was caught in mist nets with regularity. Specimens taken near Kalabakan on November 8 and 15, 1962, were in heavy molt.

=Criniger finschii= Salvadori: Finsch's Bulbul.--Specimens, 9: Cocoa Research Station: [Male] testis 5 ?4 mm., 23.1 gm., August 23, 1962, MCT 2798; [Female], 24.4 gm., August 23, 1962, MCT 2799; [Male] testis 6 ?4 mm., 24.5 gm., September 13, 1962, MCT 2914; [Female], 24.0 gm., September 13, 1962, MCT 2915; [Male] testis 4 ?3 mm., September 24, 1962, MCT 2942; [Male] testis, 6 ?5 mm., September 26, 1962, MCT 2969; [Female], September 27, 1962, MCT 2972; [Female], November 27, 1962, MCT 3341. 12 mi. N Kalabakan: [Female], October 19, 1962, heavy molt, MCT 3077.

This bulbul was common in the cocoa at the Cocoa Research Station. It fed in the company of other bulbuls in shade trees (Trema orientalis). The size of the testes of the males taken is characteristic of the beginning or ending of the breeding season, but ovaries of the females showed no signs of being in breeding condition.

According to Smythies (1960:385), this species had never been taken in North Borneo. These specimens, therefore, are the first recorded from there. Specimens previously were saved from Sarawak and Indonesian Borneo.

=Hypsipetes criniger viridis= (Bonaparte): Hairy-backed Bulbul.--Specimens, 26: Cocoa Research Station: [Male], September 26, 1962, MCT 2963; [Female], September 27, 1962, MCT 2971; [Female], November 27, 1962, MCT 3337; [Male], November 27, 1962, MCT 3356; [Female], July 7, 1963, ADG 169; [Male], June 14, 1963, ADG 139; [Male], June 12, 1963, ADG 125. 12 mi. N Kalabakan: [Female], October 13, 1962, MCT 3022; [Male], October 13, 1962, MCT 3023; [Female], October 13, 1962, MCT 3029; [Female], October 13, 1962, MCT 3033; [Male], October 14, 1962, MCT 3040; [Female], October 16, 1962, MCT 3054; [Male], October 16, 1962, MCT 3055; [Female], October 19, 1962, MCT 3081; [Female], October 19, 1962, MCT 3082; [Male], October 20, 1962, MCT 3109; [Male], October 22, 1962, MCT 3129; [Male], October 26, 1962, MCT 3162; [Male], November 11, 1962, MCT 3251; [Female], November 13, 1962, MCT 3273; [Female], November 13, 1962, MCT 3274; [Male], November 13, 1962, MCT 3275. Gum-Gum: [Female], October 3, 1963, ADG 288; [Male], October 3, 1963, ADG 289; [Male], August 12, 1963, ADG 228.

These bulbuls regularly feed on berries of Trema orientalis. I saw these bulbuls darting out after insects from branches, much as flycatchers would do, and have noticed a tendency toward flycatching in other bulbuls, but not so commonly as in this species. In using the name Hypsipetes instead of Microscelis I follow Rand and Rabor (1959:102).

=Hypsipetes malaccensis= Blyth: Streaked Bulbul.--Specimens, 4: Cocoa Research Station: [Male] testis 8 ?5 mm., 41.0 gm., August 20, 1962, MCT 2787. 12 mi. N Kalabakan: [Female], October 19, 1962, MCT 3092. 5.5 mi. SW Tenom: [Male], December 22, 1962, MCT 3497; [Male], December 22, 1962, MCT 3498.

I did not find this species common at any collecting locality. Smythies (1957:707) considered it a lowland species, but its occasional occurrence in the highlands is indicated by the specimen from Tenom.

Deignan (in Peters, 1960:291) regards Hypsipetes virescens and Hypsipetes malaccensis as specifically distinct.

=Hypsipetes charlottae perplexus= (Riley): Crested Olive Bulbul.--Specimens, 5: Cocoa Research Station: [Male] testis 5 ?3 mm., August 27, 1962, MCT 2818; [Male] testis 5 ?4 mm., September 25, 1962, MCT 2951; [Female], September 25, 1962, MCT 2952; [Male], November 27, 1962, MCT 3333; [Female] imm., 32.6 gm., July 22, 1962, MCT 2638.

This species was occasionally observed in the cocoa, where it fed on berries of Trema orientalis. The size of the testes in males taken in August suggests that the species had been breeding earlier.

=Hypsipetes flavalus connectens= (Sharpe): Ashy Bulbul.--Specimens, 7: 5.5 mi. SW Tenom: [Female], December 23, 1962, MCT 3508; [Female] largest ova 1 mm., December 17, 1962, MCT 3447; [Male], December 17, 1962, MCT 3448; [Male] testis 4 ?3 mm., December 19, 1962, MCT 3466; [Male], December 19, 1962, MCT 3467; [Male] testis 6 ?6 mm., December 20, 1962, MCT 3476; [Male] testis 5 ?4 mm., December 20, 1962, MCT 3477.

This was a common and conspicuous bird in the moss forest. Males called and sang there. The call note sounds like the mew of a cat. The Ashy Bulbul could easily be "squeaked in," at which time it approached silently. When observed in the forest it was noisy and gregarious.

=Aegithina viridissima viridissima= (Bonaparte): Green Iora.--Specimens, 7: Cocoa Research Station: [Female] largest ovum 1 mm., 13.5 gm., August 10, 1962, MCT 2755; [Male] testis 8 ?5 mm., 14.8 gm., August 10, 1962, MCT 2756; sex?, 13.2 gm., August 25, 1962, MCT 2805; [Male], 12.5 gm., September 10, 1962, MCT 2895; [Female] 13.0 gm., September 14, 1962, MCT 2921; [Female], November 27, 1962, MCT 3345. 5.5 mi. SW Tenom: [Male], December 20, 1962, MCT 3479.

In the cocoa this abundant bird usually occurred in flocks of five to 10 and fed 10 to 15 feet up in shade trees. On December 17, I saw singing males in the moss forest at 4,000 feet, 5.5 miles southwest of Tenom. This is considered a lowland species by Smythies (1957:698).

=Aegithina tiphia aequanimis= Bangs: Common Iora.--Specimens, 2: Tenom: [Male], January 5, 1963, MCT 3581; [Male], January 5, 1963, MCT 3582.

Two were netted in secondary forest near Tenom.

=Chloropsis cyanopogon cyanopogon= (Temminck): Lesser Green Leafbird.-- Specimens, 8: Cocoa Research Station: [Female], 19.8 gm., July 21, 1962, MCT 2630; [Male] testis 2 ?1 mm., 25.3 gm., July 21, 1962, MCT 2631; [Male] testis 8 ?5 mm., August 27, 1962, MCT 2819; [Female], 22.2 gm., September 14, 1962, MCT 2923; [Female], November 27, 1962, MCT 3342; [Female], November 27, 1962, MCT 3352; [Female], April 28, 1963, ADG 77; [Female], May 28, 1963, ADG 116.

It was seen regularly in the cocoa at the research station and was the most common leafbird.

=Chloropsis sonnerati zosterops= Vigors: Greater Green Leafbird.-- Specimens, 2: Cocoa Research Station: [Male] testis 3 ?2 mm., 45.8 gm., MCT 2707; [Male], 46.0 gm., August 8, 1962, MCT 2740.

It was seen many times in the cocoa.

=Irena puella criniger= Sharpe: Fairy Bluebird.--Specimens, 10: Cocoa Research Station: [Male] testis 3 ?1 mm., 63.6 gm., July 4, 1962, heavy molt, MCT 2588; [Female], 70.3 gm., July 28, 1962, MCT 2680; [Female], 69.8 gm., August 2, 1962, MCT 2711; [Male] testis 13 ?10 mm., 65.0 gm., August 2, 1962, MCT 2714; sex?, August 2, 1962, MCT 2715; sex?, 64.5 gm., August 2, 1962, MCT 2716; [Female], June 15, 1963, ADG 143; [Female], July 11, 1963, ADG 189; [Female], June 27, 1963, ADG 163. Tiger Estate: [Male], June 23, 1963, ADG 157.

This was a common species around the Research Station in the cocoa and much-disturbed primary forest.

=Erithacus cyane= (Pallas): Siberian Blue Robin.--Specimen, 1: 12 mi. N Kalabakan: [Male], November 4, 1962, MCT 3208 (netted in primary forest).

=Copsychus pyrrhopygus= (Lesson): Orange-tailed Shama.--Specimens, 9: Cocoa Research Station: [Male] testis 3 ?2 mm., July 11, 1962, MCT 2617; [Male], September 7, 1962, MCT 2885; [Female], October 3, 1962, MCT 2985; [Male], December 1, 1962, MCT 3401; [Male], November 30, 1962, MCT 3444. 12 mi. N Kalabakan: [Male] testis 5 ?3 mm., October 14, 1962 MCT 3044; [Female], November 13, 1962, MCT 3272. Oil Palm Research Station: [Male], June 20, 1963, ADG 154; [Female], August 11, 1963, ADG 222.

This bird of the primary forest was only rarely seen in secondary forest. The specimen taken on July 11, 1962, was in heavy molt with only two outermost tail feathers in evidence; there was also molt of the wing and body feathers.

=Copsychus saularis pluto= Bonaparte: Magpie-Robin.--Specimens, 3: Pintasan Agriculture Station: [Male], October 18, 1963, ADG 323. Tuaran: [Female], December 14, 1963, SCFC 219. Telipok: [Female], March 9, 1963, TM 68.

This species was recorded at Tawau in cultivated areas but no specimens were collected there. Those collected by Garcia, Chung, and Conway tended to be morphologically intermediate between C. s. adamsi and C. s. pluto.

=Copsychus stricklandi stricklandi= Motley and Dillwyn: White-rumped Shama.--Specimens, 14. Cocoa Research Station: [Male] testis 8 ?5 mm., August 28, 1962, MCT 2826; [Male] testis 11 ?6 mm., September 5, 1962, MCT 2873; [Female], November 28, 1962, MCT 3359; [Female], November 29, 1962, MCT 3389. 12 mi. N Kalabakan: [Male], October 12, 1962, MCT 3012; [Female], October 12, 1962, MCT 3013; [Female] brood patch, oviduct enlarged, October 17, 1962, MCT 3069; [Female], October 19, 1962, MCT

3078; [Female], October 26, 1962, MCT 3154. 5.5 mi. SW Tenom: [Male], December 23, 1962, MCT 3514. Ulu Balung Cocoa Estate: [Male], July 15, 1963, ADG 200. Oil Palm Research Station: [Female], August 27, 1963, ADG 263; [Female], August 28, 1963, ADG 268; [Female], October 4, 1963, ADG 291.

This species was common in the cocoa and surrounding secondary forest at Quoin Hill, but I saw it only once in the moss forest on the mountains near Tenom.

No specimen taken showed characters of or tendencies toward C. malabaricus suavis. Perhaps the zone of intergradation on the east coast is farther south than Darvel Bay, where it was placed by Smythies (1960:390).

S. D. Ripley (in Peters et al., 1964:72) considered C. stricklandi to be specifically distinct from C. malabaricus, and his opinion is accepted here.

=Enicurus leschenaulti borneensis= Sharpe: White-crowned Forktail. Specimens, 4: 12 mi. N Kalabakan: [Female] imm., October 21, 1962, MCT 3112; [Female] largest ovum 2 mm., October 27, 1962, MCT 3167; [Male], November 1, 1962, MCT 3195. Gum-Gum: [Female], September 24, 1963, ADG 282.

I saw this species only once in life, along a small, wet-weather stream. The specimens, however, were all netted in primary forest, some distance away from any stream.

Judging from measurements, these specimens are E. l. borneensis, although one would expect to find only E. l. frontalis at elevations of 600 feet. The specimen taken by Garcia at Gum-Gum was not identified to subspecies.

=Enicurus ruficapillus= Temminck: Chestnut-naped Forktail.--Specimens, 3: 12 mi. N Kalabakan: [Male], October 21, 1962, MCT 3113; [Male], November 4, 1962, MCT 3207; [Male], November 8, 1962, MCT 3231.

This bird was common along the upper Apas River at Quoin Hill. All specimens were taken in nets stretched across streams.

=Zoothera interpres interpres= (Temminck): Chestnut-headed Ground Thrush.--Specimens, 9: 12 mi. N Kalabakan: [Female], October 28, 1962, MCT 3171; [Female], October 24, 1962, MCT 3138. Kalabakan: [Female], November 17, 1962, MCT 3300. Cocoa Research Station: [Female] imm., June 10, 1963, ADG 120; [Male], June 12, 1963, ADG 130; [Female] imm., June 15, 1963, ADG 141. Oil Palm Research Station: [Male], August 15, 1963, ADG 233; [Male], August 9, 1963, ADG 217; [Male], August 27, 1963, ADG 261.

The many specimens of this species taken indicate the effectiveness of mist nets in collecting birds in tropical forest. Although Smythies (1960:398) considered this bird to be rare in Borneo, I think that it is merely shy and retiring. We never saw the species in the field and the specimens were all netted. The habitat was in primary forest, except for that of MCT 3300, which was taken in dense secondary forest. The two birds from 12 miles north of Kalabakan were taken in a net stretched across a surveyor's transect. The net was set on a hilltop and the birds hit it approximately three feet above the ground. Two of the specimens from the Cocoa Research Station are in juvenal plumage, indicating that this species probably breeds in the area.

=Cettia whiteheadi= (Sharpe): Short-tailed Bush Warbler.--Specimen, 1: 5.5 mi. SW Tenom: [Male] testis 3 ?2 mm., December 21, 1962, MCT 3488.

The specimen was netted in the moss forest, in fairly heavy secondary undergrowth.

=Prinia flaviventris= (Delessert): Yellow-bellied Wren-Warbler.--On September 2, 1962, I saw several of these wren-warblers in a grassy area near the golf course at Tawau.

=Acrocephalus arundinaceus orientalis= (Temminck and Schlegel): Great

Reed Warbler.--Specimens, 6: Tenom: [Female], December 31, 1962, MCT 3546; [Male], January 1, 1963, MCT 3555; [Male], January 2, 1963, MCT 3565; [Female], January 4, 1963, MCT 3575; [Female], January 3, 1963, MCT 3574; [Male], January 4, 1963, MCT 3579.

This species was common in the old paddy near Tenom, which has now grown up to grass and shrubs. I saw one individual also in shrubbery in Jesselton.

=Phylloscopus borealis= (Blasius): Arctic Leaf Warbler.--I saw this leaf warbler once in dense scrub in the moss forest near Tenom.

=Seicercus superciliaris schwaneri= (Blyth): White-throated Flycatcher Warbler.--Specimens, 2: 5.5 mi. SW Tenom: [Male] testis 4 ?2 mm., December 23, 1962, MCT 3510; [Female], December 23, 1962, MCT 3511.

In the moss forest this was a common bird that hopped about in the climbing bamboo and scrub.

=Orthotomus atrogularis humphreysi= Chasen and Kloss: Black-necked Tailorbird.--Specimens, 5: Cocoa Research Station: [Male] testis 4 ?2 mm., 6.5 gm., August 28, 1962, MCT 2827; [Female] oviduct enlarged, brood patch, 5.5 gm., August 28, 1962, MCT 2828; [Male] testis 4 ?2 mm., September 26, 1962, MCT 2967; [Female], November 27, 1962, MCT 3336; [Female], November 28, 1962, MCT 3375.

These birds lived in the secondary forest-edge in dense shrubbery. They were breeding at a time when most other birds seemed to have completed breeding activities; most had begun the post-breeding (prealternate) molt. On October 3, 1962, I saw two adults with two young in nondescript juvenal plumage with virtually no markings and a pale yellow color, unlike that of the adults.

=Orthotomus sericeus sericeus= Temminck: Red-headed Tailorbird.--

Specimens, 1: Cocoa Research Station: [Female] with large ovum, 10.8 gm., August 11, 1962, MCT 2770.

The bird was uncommon at the research station. The one specimen was from the cocoa. I saw two others in secondary growth on the edge of the forest. Possibly this species, like the preceding one, was approaching full breeding activity.

=Orthotomus sepium borneonensis= Salvadori: Ashy Tailorbird.--Specimens, 8: Cocoa Research Station: [Female] vascular brood patch, oviduct enlarged with one possible collapsed follicle, 7.8 gm., August 22, 1962, MCT 2797; [Female] imm., 8.0 gm., August 28, 1962, MCT 2829; [Male], 8.8 gm., September 10, 1962, MCT 2896; [Male], 8.5 gm., September 10, 1962, MCT 2897; [Male] testis 5 ?3 mm., 8.5 gm., September 11, 1962, MCT 2901; [Female] largest ova 3 mm., 8.5 gm., September 11, 1962, MCT 2902. Tiger Estate: [Female], October 11, 1962, MCT 3000. 5.5 mi. SW Tenom: [Female], December 20, 1962, MCT 3486.

This was the most common tailorbird in the Quoin Hill area. Indications were that the species was also breeding (see O. sericeus). Besides the above localities, I observed it 12 miles north of Kalabakan. A male was heard singing on September 11, 1962; the song was simple and on an ascending scale. The specimen taken near Tenom was growing new tail feathers.

=Rhipidura perlata= S. Muller: Spotted Fantail Flycatcher.--Specimens, 19: Cocoa Research Station: [Female] largest ova 2 mm., July 11, 1962, MCT 2618; [Male] testis 6 ?5 mm., 15.1 gm., July 23, 1962, MCT 2645; [Female], 13.2 gm., August 13, 1962, MCT 2776; [Female], 12.4 gm., August 20, 1962, MCT 2785; [Male], June 12, 1963, ADG 129. 12 mi. N Kalabakan: [Male], October 13, 1962, MCT 3021; [Male], October 16, 1962, MCT 3056; [Female], October 16, 1962, MCT 3057; [Male], October 16, 1962, MCT 3111; [Female], October 24, 1962, MCT 3141; [Male], October 24, 1962, MCT 3146; [Male], October 24, 1962, MCT 3148; sex?, October 26, 1962, MCT 3165; [Male], October 27, 1962, MCT 3168; [Male], October 27, 1962, MCT 3169; sex?, October 30,

1962, MCT 3197. Ulu Balung Cocoa Estate: [Female], July 13, 1963, ADG 198; [Female], July 24, 1963, ADG 214. Oil Palm Research Station: sex?, August 15, 1963, ADG 243.

This bird was one of the most common in the lower story of the primary forest. On July 23, 1962, many males were performing courtship displays at Quoin Hill.

=Rhipidura javanica longicauda= Wallace: Pied Fan-tailed Flycatcher.-- Specimens, 3: Tawau: sex?, September 2, 1962, MCT 2863. Telipok: [Female], February 9, 1963, TM 28. Tuaran: sex?, December 14, 1963, SCFC 19.

On Karindingen Island this was the only passerine bird seen. It was confined to the lowlands and never was seen in localities more than a few feet above sea level.

=Culicicapa ceylonensis ceylonensis= (Swainson): Gray-headed Flycatcher.-- Specimens, 6: Cocoa Research Station: [Male], 8.0 gm., August 4, 1962, MCT 2726; sex?, August 20, 1962, 8.6 gm., MCT 2784. 12 mi. N Kalabakan: [Female]?, October 12, 1962, MCT 3018; [Male], October 13, 1962, MCT 3024; [Male] testis 4 ?4 mm., October 28, 1962, MCT 3179. 5.5 mi. SW Tenom: [Male], December 20, 1962, MCT 3483.

This bird of the primary forest and primary-secondary forest ecotone was common at all three principal collecting stations.

=Muscicapa sibirica= Gmelin: Sooty Flycatcher.--Specimens, 2: Cocoa Research Station: [Male], 10.0 gm., August 25, 1962, MCT 2811; [Male], July 8, 1963, ADG 174.

Several small "brown" flycatchers which could not be assigned to species were observed at Quoin Hill and Kalabakan. The specimen taken by Garcia is of interest as it was taken on a date extremely early for a migrant. Garcia's specimen (not the other) also presented problems of identification and its assignment to this species is tentative.

=Muscicapa latirostris latirostris= Raffles: Brown Flycatcher.--Specimen, 1: Cocoa Research Station: [Female], September 26, 1962, MCT 2965.

=Muscicapa cyanomelana cyanomelana= Temminck: Blue and White Flycatcher.--Specimen, 1: Cocoa Research Station: [Male], November 27, 1962, MCT 3335.

The specimen, netted in the cocoa, apparently provides the only record from the east coast of Borneo (see Smythies, 1957:742).

=Muscicapa concreta everetti= (Sharpe): White-tailed Blue Flycatcher.-- Specimens, 6: 12 mi. N Kalabakan: [Male], October 15, 1962, MCT 3045; [Male], November 1, 1962, MCT 3199; [Female], November 8, 1962, MCT 3229; [Male], November 8, 1962, MCT 3230. 5.5 mi. SW Tenom: [Male], December 19, 1962, MCT 3465; [Female], December 23, 1962, MCT 3516.

This species seems to be confined to the primary forest, and was common at both localities listed. Smythies (1960:444) thought it resided primarily at elevations of 2,000 to 4,000 feet, occasionally occurring near sea level. This flycatcher seems to prefer the understory of the forest, where it was observed sitting on bare limbs and darting out after insects.

=Muscicapa unicolor infuscata= (Hartert): Pale Blue Flycatcher.--Specimens, 2: 12 mi. N Kalabakan: [Male] by plumage, October 31, 1962, MCT 3189; [Female], November 12, 1962, MCT 3556.

This flycatcher was seen only in primary forest, on the above dates. The birds collected appear to provide the only definitive records for North Borneo (cf. Smythies, 1960:445), although Mary Norman observed the species once at Quoin Cocoa Estate on an unspecified date (Smythies, 1963:281).

=Muscicapa turcosa rupatensis= Oberholser: Malaysian Blue Flycatcher.--

Specimen, 1: Tiger Estate: [Female], November 25, 1962, MCT 3320.

=Muscicapa caerulata caerulata= (Bonaparte): Large-billed Blue Flycatcher.--
Specimens, 10: Ulu Balung Cocoa Estate: [Male], July 10, 1963, ADG 185. 12
mi. N Kalabakan: [Male], October 19, 1962, MCT 3076; [Male], October 24,
1962, MCT 3144; [Male], October 26, 1962, MCT 3160; [Female], October 28,
1962, MCT 3170; [Female], November 8, 1962, MCT 3232; [Male], November
13, 1962, MCT 3266. Oil Palm Research Station: [Female], August 12, 1963,
ADG 223; [Female], August 16, 1963, ADG 244; [Male], August 19, 1963, ADG
252.

This was the most common "blue" flycatcher at Kalabakan. It was recorded
at Quoin Hill only by Garcia. The record by Smythies (1963:281) seems open
to question as no specimen was preserved.

=Muscicapa venusta= Deignan: Bornean Blue Flycatcher.--Specimens, 6:
Cocoa Research Station: [Male], September 24, 1962, MCT 2939; [Male], June
12, 1963, ADG 128. 12 mi. N Kalabakan: [Male], October 12, 1962, MCT 3014;
[Male], October 19, 1962, MCT 3089. Oil Palm Research Station: [Female],
August 10, 1963, ADG 218. Kinabatangan: sex?, October 15, 1963, ADG 309.

The "blue" flycatcher of the Quoin Hill area was observed several times in
the primary forest and primary forest edge. On July 14, 1962, I saw a male
and a female of M. venusta bathing in a shallow stream in the deep forest.
They fluttered their wings in the water and then flew to a nearby fallen log
and preened for several minutes.

=Muscicapa rufigastra rufigastra= Raffles: Mangrove Blue Flycatcher.--
Specimen, 1: Tuaran: [Male], December 14, 1963, SCFC 33.

=Muscicapa dumetoria mulleri= Blyth: Orange-breasted Flycatcher.--
Specimens, 5: Cocoa Research Station: [Male], 11.8 gm., July 25, 1962, MCT
2661; [Female], November 1, 1962, MCT 3198; [Male] testis 3 ?2 mm.,
November 11, 1962, MCT 3246; [Male] testis 5 ?4 mm., November 28, 1962,

MCT 3384. 5.5 mi. SW Tenom: [Male], December 25, 1962, MCT 3531.

This species was seen only in the understory of primary forest. On November 10, I watched a male and female feeding about three feet above the ground in the undergrowth. They sat on small vines and plants and darted out after insects. I never observed this species more than 20 feet above the ground.

=Muscicapa narcissina= Temminck: Black and Yellow Flycatcher.--Specimens, 2: Cocoa Research Station: [Female], November 27, 1962, MCT 3331. 5.5 mi. SW Tenom: [Male], December 20, 1962, MCT 3484.

The two specimens were taken in nets in the primary forest. They cannot presently be assigned with certainty to subspecies.

=Rhinomyias umbratilis= (Strickland): White-throated Jungle Flycatcher.-- Specimens, 19: Cocoa Research Station: [Female], 16.7 gm., July 25, 1962, MCT 2662; [Male] testis 6 ?5 mm., 20.7 gm., July 25, 1962, MCT 2663; [Female], 17.9 gm., July 31, 1962, MCT 2686; [Female], September 29, 1962, MCT 2974; [Male], July 8, 1963, ADG 175. 12 mi. N Kalabakan: [Male], October 10, 1962, MCT 2993; [Female], October 13, 1962, MCT 3027; [Male], October 13, 1962, MCT 3031; [Male], October 14, 1962, MCT 3036; [Male], October 16, 1962, MCT 3053; [Male], October 16, 1962, MCT 3058; [Male], October 18, 1962, MCT 3074; [Female], October 20, 1962, MCT 3107; [Male], October 23, 1962, MCT 3132; [Male], October 25, 1962, MCT 3149; [Female], October 28, 1962, MCT 3174. Ulu Balung Cocoa Estate: [Female], July 11, 1963, ADG 195; [Female], July 12, 1963, ADG 196; [Female], July 19, 1963, ADG 212.

This abundant species at Quoin Hill and Kalabakan was chiefly an inhabitant of primary forest.

On July 31, I observed this species singing at Quoin Hill. One sang with its mouth closed and sounded much farther away than it actually was. The song has seven notes on a descending scale. Birds observed on September 27 were in heavy molt and one specimen lacked tail feathers.

=Philentoma pyrrhoptera pyrrhoptera= (Temminck): Chestnut-winged Monarch Flycatcher.--Specimens, 10: 12 mi. N Kalabakan: [Male], October 10, 1962, MCT 2992; [Female], October 15, 1962, MCT 3048; [Male], October 20, 1962, MCT 3100; [Male], October 20, 1962, MCT 3105; [Female], November 11, 1962, MCT 3244; [Female], November 16, 1962, MCT 3291. Ulu Balung Cocoa Estate: [Male], July 9, 1963, ADG 180; [Male], July 9, 1963, ADG 181; [Male], July 24, 1963, ADG 215; [Female], July 11, 1963, ADG 192.

The species was common at Kalabakan. Garcia took a few at Quoin Hill, but I observed the species there only once.

=Philentoma velata caesia= (Lesson): Maroon-breasted Monarch Flycatcher.--Specimens, 7: Cocoa Research Station: [Female], 25.0 gm., August 4, 1962, MCT 2725; [Male], 27.2 gm., August 20, 1962, MCT 2783; [Male], September 5, 1962, MCT 2872. 12 mi. N Kalabakan: [Female], October 22, 1962, MCT 3126; sex? ([Female] by plumage), October 29, 1962, MCT 3182; [Female], November 3, 1962, MCT 3205. 5.5 mi. SW Tenom: [Male], December 26, 1962, MCT 3536.

At Quoin Hill this was a bird of the primary forest. The species was common in the moss forest above Tenom.

=Hypothymis azurea prophata= Oberholser: Black-naped Blue Monarch Flycatcher.--Specimens, 18: Cocoa Research Station: [Female], 10.8 gm., August 10, 1962, MCT 2754; [Male], 15.2 gm., August 28, 1962, MCT 2834; [Male] testis 6 ?4 mm., 11.1 gm., September 6, 1962, MCT 2876; sex? September 14, 1962, MCT 2922; [Male], November 1, 1962, MCT 3200; [Male], November 7, 1962, MCT 3221; [Male], November 10, 1962, MCT 3242; [Male], November 20, 1962, MCT 3373; [Female], November 28, 1962, MCT 3374; [Male] testis 5 ?3 mm., December 1, 1962, MCT 3412; [Female], December 2, 1962, MCT 3427. 5.5 mi. SW Tenom: [Male], December 22, 1962,

MCT 3504; [Male], December 23, 1962, MCT 3509. Cocoa Research Station: [Female], April 30, 1963, ADG 95; [Female], June 19, 1963, ADG 1551. Ulu Balung Cocoa Estate: [Male], July 11, 1963, ADG 194; Oil Palm Research Station: [Male], August 10, 1963, ADG 220; [Female], August 13, 1963, ADG 232.

This seemingly ubiquitous bird occurred in primary forest and cocoa. A specimen taken on September 14, 1962, was still in heavy molt.

=Terpsiphone paradisi borneensis= (Hartert): Paradise Flycatcher.-- Specimens, 6: Cocoa Research Station: [Male] testis 9 ?5 mm., July 11, 1962, MCT 2616; [Male] testis 2 ?1 mm., 21.2 gm., August 3, 1962, MCT 2719; [Female], June 10, 1963, ADG 119. 12 mi. N Kalabakan: [Male], October 19, 1962, MCT 3090; [Female], November 10, 1962, MCT 3240. Oil Palm Research Station: [Female], August 24, 1963, ADG 258.

At Quoin Hill this species was common in primary forest. One of the males (MCT 2719) was rust-colored. It and similar rufous males may be immature (see Owen, 1963:235).

=Pachycephala whiteheadi homeyeri= (Blasius): Whitehead's Thick-head.-- Specimens, 2: Siamil Island: [Female], September 19, 1962, MCT 2931; [Male], September 19, 1962, MCT 2932.

The thick-heads were by far the most common passerine bird in the relict forest on Siamil Island, being quite tame and easily approached. They generally spent most of their time sitting on branches of forest vines and bushes in the understory and were never observed in the upper story. McGregor (1910:604) describes the species as: "Common on Tawi Tawi, less so in Sulu. A deep woods bird; tame and easily shot. Feeds on insects, and usually keeps some distance above the ground."

The two specimens recorded above provide the first record of this species from Borneo, the previously known range being confined to the Philippine

Islands. My material closely resembled the subspecies found on Tawi-Tawi and here is assigned to P. w. homeyeri.

=Motacilla caspica melanope= Pallas: Gray Wagtail.--Specimen, 1: Cocoa Research Station: [Female], October 4, 1962, MCT 2991.

I saw this migrant first at the research station on August 25, 1962, along a dirt road, and it was subsequently seen many times along logging roads in secondary forest.

=Artamus leucorhynchus leucorhynchus= Linnaeus: White-breasted Swallow Shrike.--Specimens, 2: Tuaran: sex?, December 6, 1963, SCFC F13; [Female], December 7, 1963, SCFC F15.

=Lanius cristatus lucionensis= Linnaeus: Brown Shrike.--Specimen, 1: Tuaran: [Male], January 12, 1963, MCT 3593.

One bird was observed near our sulap 12 miles north of Kalabakan on October 22 and 26, 1962. The specimen was netted in a paddy field and others were seen at Tuaran.

=Lanius tigrinus= Drapiez: Thick-billed Shrike.--Specimens, 2: Tiger Estate: [Male], November 25, 1962, MCT 3316. Cocoa Research Station: [Female], November 29, 1962, MCT 3383.

The specimen taken on November 29, was netted in a small clearing in primary forest.

=Aplonis panayensis strigatus= (Horsfield): Glossy Starling.--Specimens, 2: Tiger Estate: [Female], October 11, 1962, MCT 3001; [Female], November 25, 1962, MCT 3322. Tuaran: [Female], March 21, 1963, ADG 35; sex?, December 1, 1963, EJHB 616.

This species was in the lowlands around Semporna, Siamil Island, Brantian

Estate, and Tawau.

=Gracula religiosa religiosa= Linnaeus: Talking Myna.--Specimens, 3: Tiger Estate: [Female], October 11, 1962, MCT 3020. Cocoa Research Station: [Male], May 28, 1963, ADG 114. Gum-Gum: [Female], September 9, 1963, ADG 277.

This was a common bird at Quoin Hill but was not seen elsewhere by me. It frequented the dead trees in the cocoa.

=Anthreptes simplex= (S. Muller): Plain-colored Sunbird.--Specimens, 6: Cocoa Research Station: [Female] imm., 8.0 gm., August 11, 1962, MCT 2768; [Male] imm., 10.0 gm., August 11, 1962, MCT 2769; [Male], 7.0 gm., September 6, 1962, MCT 2878; [Male], September 25, 1962, MCT 2959; [Female], November 27, 1962, MCT 3332; [Male], November 27, 1962, MCT 3343.

This common bird at Quoin Hill frequented flowers of the Tree Cassava. Trees of that species were shade trees in the cocoa.

=Anthreptes malacensis= ssp. (Scopoli): Brown-throated Sunbird.--Specimens, 2: Tenom: [Male], January 3, 1963, MCT 3573; [Male] testis 5 ?4 mm., January 4, 1963, MCT 3576.

One of the specimens (MCT 3576) was molting into adult male plumage; the size of its testes suggests that this bird was also coming into breeding condition, all of which seemingly lends support to Chasen's (1939:401) suspicion that the species has an eclipse plumage. Lacking specimens in breeding plumage, I was unable to determine the subspecific affinities of the population at Tenom.

This species was observed also on Siamil Island.

=Anthreptes rhodolaema= Shelley: Rufous-throated Sunbird.--Specimens, 14:

Cocoa Research Station: [Male] testis 3 ?3 mm., 12.5 gm., August 9, 1962, MCT 2742; [Male] testis 5 ?3 mm., 15.0 gm., August 9, 1962, MCT 2743; [Female], 13.5 gm., August 9, 1962, MCT 2744; [Female] imm., 12.7 gm., August 9, 1962, MCT 2745; [Male] testis 3 ?2 mm., 13.5 gm., August 10, 1962, MCT 2749; [Male], 13.0 gm., August 10, 1962, MCT 2750; [Female], 12.0 gm., August 10, 1962, MCT 2751; [Female] imm., 10.8 gm., August 13, 1962, MCT 2775; [Male], September 4, 1962, MCT 2869; [Female] largest ova 3 mm., oviduct enlarged, 12.0 gm., September 12, 1962, MCT 2905; [Female], November 27, 1962, MCT 3350; [Male], November 27, 1962, MCT 3351; [Male], November 27, 1962, MCT 3355.

The Rufous-throated Sunbirds were the most common sunbirds at the Cocoa Research Station. They seemed to prefer foraging about flowers of the Tree Cassava. The stomachs of those examined contained insects. The absence of A. malacensis suggests that these two species are mutually exclusive.

=Anthreptes singalensis borneana= (Kloss): Ruby-cheeked Sunbird.-- Specimens, 3: Cocoa Research Station: [Male], 8.0 gm., August 23, 1962, MCT 2801; [Male], November 29, 1962, MCT 3385; [Female], 8.4 gm., August 10, 1962, MCT 2752.

This species seemed to prefer secondary forest or cocoa as a habitat and was an uncommon bird at Quoin Hill.

=Nectarinia sperata= (Linnaeus): Van Hasselt's Sunbird.--Fred Dunn saw a male in secondary forest near the Cocoa Research Station.

=Nectarinia jugularis= (Linnaeus): Yellow-breasted Sunbird.--This sunbird was abundant in the coconut palms at Siamil Island. The species was observed also at exotic flowering plants in Tawau.

=Nectarinia hypogrammica hypogrammica= S. Muller: Purple-naped Sunbird.- -Specimens, 10: Cocoa Research Station: [Female], November 27, 1962, MCT

3334: [Male], July 7, 1963, ADG 167. 12 mi. N Kalabakan: [Male] testis 3 ?5 mm., October 14, 1962, MCT 3035; [Male], October 15, 1962, MCT 3047; [Male], October 23, 1962, MCT 3133; [Male], October 24, 1962, MCT 3145; [Male], November 2, 1962, MCT 3203; [Female], November 15, 1962, MCT 3287. Oil Palm Research Station: [Female], August 16, 1963, ADG 247; [Male], August 27, 1963, ADG 262.

This common species of secondary forest at Quoin Hill seems to prefer spiders and various insects for food. I saw one bird removing dead leaves from a tree and picking out the spiders that had taken over the curled leaves as shelters. I also saw birds of this species hover before spiderwebs and remove the spiders.

A specimen taken on November 15, 1962, was in heavy molt.

=Aethopyga mystacalis= (Temminck): Scarlet Sunbird.--Specimen, 1: Cocoa Research Station: [Male], 6.0 gm., September 12, 1962, MCT 2903.

This specimen was molting from a drab to an adult type male plumage. I saw this species only one other time at Quoin Hill, but on December 26 I saw two males feeding among epiphytic plants in the moss forest above Tenom. The condition of the specimen's plumage prevented its identification to subspecies (presumably A. m. temmincki).

=Aethopyga siparaja= (Raffles): Yellow-backed Sunbird.--Specimens, 3: Tawau: [Male] testis 5 ?5 mm., September 2, 1962, MCT 2861. Tiger Estate: [Male], October 11, 1962, MCT 2999. Oil Palm Research Station: [Female], August 13, 1963, ADG 231.

This sunbird was common around flowers at Kalabakan and Brantian Estate.

Unfortunately, I lack enough specimens to make a subspecific identification. The specimen from Tawau differs from A. s. siparaja, however, only in having darker wings; it closely resembles the type and the series that Oberholser used when describing A. s. ochrapyrrha.

=Arachnothera longirostris buttikoferi= van Oort: Little Spiderhunter.--
Specimens, 58: Cocoa Research Station: [Male], 16.2 gm., August 13, 1962,
MCT 2777; [Male], 15.6 gm., August 22, 1962, MCT 2796; [Male] testis 6 ?4
mm., 16.0 gm., September 13, 1962, MCT 2913; [Female], December 1, 1962,
MCT 3399; [Male] testis 4 ?3 mm., December 2, 1962, MCT 3431; [Male],
November 27, 1962, MCT 3347; [Female], November 27, 1962, MCT 3348;
[Male], November 28, 1962, MCT 3366; [Male], November 28, 1962, MCT
3367; [Female], November 28, 1962, MCT 3368; [Female], November 28,
1962, MCT 3369; [Male], November 28, 1962, MCT 3370; [Female],
November 28, 1962, MCT 3371; [Male], November 28, 1962, MCT 3372;
[Male], November 29, 1962, MCT 3386; [Male], December 1, 1962, MCT 3397;
[Male], December 1, 1962, MCT 3398; [Female], December 2, 1962, MCT
3430; [Female]?, November 30, 1962, MCT 3443; [Female], April 26, 1962,
ADG 60; [Male], April 27, 1963, ADG 70; [Male], April 27, 1962, ADG 73;
[Male], April 18, 1963, ADG 78; [Male], April 28, 1963, ADG 80; [Male], April
29, 1963, ADG 86; [Male], April 29, 1963, ADG 87; [Male], April 30, 1962, ADG
93. 12 mi. N Kalabakan: [Female], October 16, 1962, MCT 3050; [Male],
October 16, 1962, MCT 3051; [Male] testis 4 ?2 mm., October 18, 1962, MCT
3073; [Female], October 17, 1962, MCT 3064; [Male] testis 7 ?5 mm., October
19, 1962, MCT 3079; [Female], October 19, 1962, MCT 3093; [Male], October
21, 1962, MCT 3120; [Male], October 23, 1962, MCT 3134; [Male] testis
enlarged, October 25, 1962, MCT 3150; [Male] testis 7 ?5 mm., October 26,
1962, MCT 3156; [Female], October 28, 1962, MCT 3173; [Male], November 2,
1962, MCT 3204; [Male], November 4, 1962, MCT 3209; [Male] testis 5 ?4
mm., November 4, 1962, MCT 3210; [Male] testis 2 ?1 mm., November 6,
1962, MCT 3214; [Female], November 11, 1962, MCT 3252. Kalabakan:
[Female], November 15, 1962, MCT 3278; [Female] 2 eggs in oviduct, ovary
enlarged, brood patch, November 15, 1962, MCT 3279; [Female] brood patch,
two collapsed follicles, November 15, 1962, MCT 3280; [Male] testis 7 ?6 mm.,
November 15, 1962, MCT 3281; [Female] brood patch, egg in oviduct, largest
ovum 6 mm., November 15, 1962, MCT 3286; [Male] testis 7 ?6 mm.,
November 16, 1962, MCT 3290; [Male] testis 3 ?2 mm., November 16, 1962,

MCT 3294; [Female], November 16, 1962, MCT 3295; [Male] testis 6 ?3 mm., November 17, 1962, MCT 3297; [Male] testis 5 ?5 mm., November 17, 1962, MCT 3298; [Female], November 17, 1962, MCT 3299. 5.5 mi. SW Tenom: [Female], December 26, 1962, MCT 3538. Gum-Gum: [Male], October 4, 1963, ADG 290; [Female], October 5, 1963, ADG 294; [Female], October 5, 1963, ADG 295.

This was the most common of all the spiderhunters, and was found at all localities. It was readily taken in mist nets. Unlike most birds, these spiderhunters become quite agitated in nets, and within a few minutes usually strangle themselves.

From October 16 through November 11, I took several specimens 12 miles north of Kalabakan, but only one in breeding condition. On November 15, I moved 12 miles back to Kalabakan from an elevation of 600 feet to an elevation of 50 feet. As can be seen from the specimen-data, nearly all the females then collected either had nests with eggs or were approaching oviposition. The specimens were all taken in nets in an area approximately 200 feet square. On November 20 at the Brantian Estate a bird sitting on a branch six inches up in secondary forest jumped down to the ground and fed on unknown material.

=Arachnothera crassirostris= (Reichenbach): Thick-billed Spiderhunter.-- Specimen, 1: Cocoa Research Station: [Female], 14.8 gm., August 9, 1962, MCT 2746.

This spiderhunter was recorded on the basis of one specimen and one sight record. One seen in secondary forest would dart out from its perch on a limb, hover near the end of a branch, and then return to its perch. No flowers were visible and I assumed that the bird was catching insects.

=Arachnothera flavigaster= (Eyton): Greater Yellow-eared Spiderhunter.-- Specimens, 9: Cocoa Research Station: [Female] imm., 36.3 gm., August 21, 1962, MCT 2789; [Female] imm., 38.4 gm., August 21, 1962, MCT 2790;

[Female], 38.4 gm., August 22, 1962, MCT 2795; [Female] brood patch, largest ova 2 mm., November 27, 1962, MCT 3330; [Male], November 28, 1962, MCT 3359; [Male] testis 7 ?6 mm., November 29, 1962, MCT 3379; [Male], November 30, 1962, MCT 3395; [Female], April 27, 1963, ADG 66; [Female], April 27, 1963, ADG 67.

This species was met with only at Quoin Hill, where it was common around the abaca and wild bananas. The primary diet seemed to be pollen, nectar, and spiders. I found it easy to differentiate from the next species in the field (see below).

=Arachnothera chrysogenys harrissoni= Deignan: Lesser Yellow-eared Spiderhunter.--Specimens, 4: Cocoa Research Station: [Female], 23.5 gm., August 21, 1962, MCT 2788; [Male], April 27, 1963, ADG 68; [Male], April 30, 1963, ADG 92; [Male], May 27, 1963, ADG 113.

I observed this species at Quoin Hill only once, but Garcia took three specimens at the same locality. He labels his specimens as taken in primary forest. I never saw the species there and took my one specimen in the abaca, where the bird was eating spiders, nectar, and pollen. The chief characters distinguishing this species from A. flavigaster were the tuft of yellow feathers on the side of the head and the narrow eye ring in A. chrysogenys.

=Arachnothera affinis pars= Riley: Gray-breasted Spiderhunter.--Specimens, 27: Cocoa Research Station: [Male], 27.2 gm., August 13, 1962, MCT 2771; [Female], 22.2 gm., August 13, 1962, MCT 2772; [Female] imm., 21.1 gm., August 13, 1962, MCT 2773; [Male], 29.2 gm., August 13, 1962, MCT 2774; [Male], 27.0 gm., August 21, 1962, MCT 2791; [Male], 26.6 gm., August 21, 1962, MCT 2792; [Male], April 27, 1963, ADG 65; [Female] imm., May 1, 1963, ADG 99; [Male], June 12, 1963, ADG 126; [Male], June 20, 1963, ADG 154-B. 12 mi. N Kalabakan: [Female], October 15, 1962, MCT 3046; [Female], October 24, 1962, MCT 3139. Cocoa Research Station: [Male] testis 3 ?2 mm., November 27, 1962, MCT 3327; [Female], November 27, 1962, MCT 3328; [Female], November 27, 1962, MCT 3329; [Female], November 27, 1962, MCT

3338; [Male] testis 5 ?4 mm., November 27, 1962, MCT 3339; [Male], November 28, 1962, MCT 3363; [Female], November 28, 1962, MCT 3364; [Male], November 28, 1962, MCT 3365; [Female], November 28, 1962, MCT 3366; [Female], November 29, 1962, MCT 3390; [Male] testis enlarged, November 29, 1962, MCT 3391; [Female]?, November 29, 1962, MCT 3392; [Male], December 1, 1962, MCT 3393; [Male], December 2, 1962, MCT 3429; [Male], November 30, 1962, MCT 3442.

This bird was fairly common at Quoin Hill in the abaca and wild bananas and, at Kalabakan, in primary forest. Its feeding habits are the same as those of the preceding species. The order of abundance of the spiderhunters is probably best shown by the number of each species taken: Arachnothera longirostris, 58; A. affinis, 27; A. flavigaster, 9; A. chrysogenys, 4; A. crassirostris, 1.

=Prionichilus xanthopygius= (Salvadori): Yellow-rumped Flowerpecker.-- Specimens, 7: Cocoa Research Station: [Male] testis 5 ?5 mm., 8.9 gm., August 23, 1962, MCT 2800; [Female] largest ova 3 mm., oviduct enlarged, 10.2 gm., September 13, 1962, MCT 2910; [Female] imm., 9.7 gm., September 13, 1962, MCT 2911; [Male] testis 3 ?2 mm., 9.5 gm., September 13, 1962, MCT 2912; [Female] imm., 7.0 gm., September 14, 1962, MCT 2920; [Male] testis 6 ?4 mm., vas deferens enlarged, September 26, 1962, MCT 2966; [Male], November 27, 1962, MCT 3344.

This species did not appear at Quoin Hill until August 23. The gonads of most of the adults taken from that time on appeared to be regressing from breeding condition, and several immatures were taken also, suggesting that the breeding season was over. The birds seemed to be attracted, with bulbuls, to the tree Trema orientalis.

=Prionichilus maculatus maculatus= (Temminck): Yellow-throated Flowerpecker.--Specimen, 1: 12 mi. N Kalabakan: [Male], October 19, 1962, MCT 3094.

I observed this flowerpecker once at Quoin Hill, in much-disturbed primary forest, but was unable to secure a specimen. Twelve miles north of Kalabakan it was found in primary forest.

=Dicaeum chrysorrheum= Temminck: Yellow-vented Flowerpecker.--I observed one feeding about 50 feet high among epiphytic plants in the moss forest 5.5 miles north of Tenom.

=Dicaeum monticolum= Sharpe: Black-sided Flowerpecker.--Specimen, 1: 5.5 mi. SW Tenom: [Male] testis 5 ?3 mm., December 17, 1962, MCT 3449.

I saw this flowerpecker once, in the moss forest above Tenom. Treatment of this species as monotypic follows the revision of Salomonsen (1961:17).

=Dicaeum cruentatum= (Linnaeus): Scarlet-backed Flowerpecker.--Along the seashore near Tawau this species fed in flowering trees. Males were pugnacious and persistently chased what appeared to be females.

=Dicaeum trigonostigma dayakanum= Chasen and Kloss: Orange-bellied Flowerpecker.--Specimen, 1: 5.5 mi. SW Tenom: [Male], December 23, 1962, MCT 3507.

This flowerpecker was found only in the moss forest above Tenom, where it was seen numerous times feeding among the epiphytic plants.

=Zosterops everetti tahanensis= Ogilvie-Grant: Everett's White-eye.-- Specimens, 9: Cocoa Research Station: [Female], August 8, 1962, MCT 2734; [Male] testis 4 ?3 mm., August 8, 1962, MCT 2735; [Female], 8.6 gm., August 11, 1962, MCT 2757; [Female], 7.8 gm., August 11, 1962, MCT 2758; [Female] imm., 7.9 gm., August 11, 1962, MCT 2759; [Female], 8.2 gm., August 11, 1962, MCT 2760; [Male], 7.8 gm., August 11, 1962, MCT 2761; [Male] imm., August 11, 1962, MCT 2762; [Male] imm., 7.8 gm., August 11, 1962, MCT 2764.

At the Cocoa Research Station flocks of 20 to 40 birds were seen daily, feeding in the cocoa trees. Only once was this species seen away from the cocoa trees; this was in secondary forest where the birds were feeding in a tree about 30 feet tall. They move in flocks and are noisy.

Smythies (1960:485) states that this species occurs from the Poi Range up to the lower slopes of Kinabalu. This is apparently the first record from eastern Borneo.

=Lonchura fuscans= (Cassin): Dusky Munia.--Specimens, 11. Cocoa Research Station: [Female], July 6, 1962, MCT 2603; [Female], September 1, 1962, MCT 2847; [Male] testis 7 ?6 mm., September 1, 1962, MCT 2848; [Male] testis enlarged, September 24, 1962, MCT 2943. Tenom: [Female], January 6, 1962, MCT 3584; [Female], January 6, 1963, MCT 3585; [Male] testis enlarged, January 6, 1963, MCT 3586; [Female] several collapsed follicles, old brood patch, January 6, 1963, MCT 3587; [Female] imm., January 6, 1963, MCT 3588; [Female], January 6, 1963, MCT 3590; [Male] testis enlarged, January 6, 1963, MCT 3591.

In contrast to L. malacca, this species was commonly found in secondary forest away from cultivated fields. It was common at Quoin Hill and Kalabakan. On July 18, 1962, a pair was observed building a nest near Kalabakan, in a native kampong under the eave of a house. There the birds were fastening the nest to the palm thatching about 20 feet up and nearly over the door. Another pair was nesting, close to the same house, about eight feet up in a citrus tree. In Kalabakan proper, I saw a pair with fledgling young in a croton bush about six feet from the door of a house, on November 15, 1962. This nest was about seven feet up.

=Lonchura malacca= (Linnaeus): Chestnut Munia.--Specimens, 6: Tawau: [Female] imm., September 2, 1962, MCT 2862. Tenom: [Male], January 6, 1963, MCT 3589. Tuaran: [Female], January 12, 1963, MCT 3594; [Female], January 12, 1963, MCT 3595; hermaphrodite, testis 8 ?5 mm., largest ovum of ovary 2 mm., January 12, 1963, MCT 3596; [Female], January 12, 1963, MCT

3597.

This was a common bird in the lowlands away from forest. I observed it feeding on lawns in Tawau. A pair was building a nest on July 19, 1962, in an ironwood tree about 10 feet above the ground. The nest was typically ball-shaped with a side entrance. This species appears to stay in age groups when it flocks, as evidenced by the large flocks of young in first-year plumage.

The hermaphroditic specimen was of some interest, since the ovary and testis both seemed to be enlarged.

###